Digital and Cybersecurity Governance Around the World

Other titles in Annals of Corporate Governance

Enterprise Foundations: Law, Taxation, Governance, and Performance
Steen Thomsen and Nikolaos Kavadis
ISBN: 978-1-68083-942-5

Beyond ESG: Reforming Capitalism and Social Democracy
Marcel Boyer
ISBN: 978-1-68083-894-7

The Social Purpose of the Modern Business Corporation
Peter J. Buckley
ISBN: 978-1-68083-874-9

Decentralized Autonomous Organizations: Internal Governance and External Legal Design
Wulf A. Kaal
ISBN: 978-1-68083-798-8

Decentralized Corporate Governance via Blockchain Technology
Wulf A. Kaal
ISBN: 978-1-68083-676-9

Digital and Cybersecurity Governance Around the World

Bob Zukis
Digital Directors Network, and
USC Marshall School of Business
bob@digitaldirectors.network

Boston — Delft

Annals of Corporate Governance

Published, sold and distributed by:
now Publishers Inc.
PO Box 1024
Hanover, MA 02339
United States
Tel. +1-781-985-4510
www.nowpublishers.com
sales@nowpublishers.com

Outside North America:
now Publishers Inc.
PO Box 179
2600 AD Delft
The Netherlands
Tel. +31-6-51115274

The preferred citation for this publication is

B. Zukis. *Digital and Cybersecurity Governance Around the World*. Annals of Corporate Governance, vol. 7, no. 1, pp. 1–92, 2022.

ISBN: 978-1-63828-046-0
© 2022 B. Zukis

All rights reserved. No part of this publication may be reproduced, stored in a retrieval system, or transmitted in any form or by any means, mechanical, photocopying, recording or otherwise, without prior written permission of the publishers.

Photocopying. In the USA: This journal is registered at the Copyright Clearance Center, Inc., 222 Rosewood Drive, Danvers, MA 01923. Authorization to photocopy items for internal or personal use, or the internal or personal use of specific clients, is granted by now Publishers Inc for users registered with the Copyright Clearance Center (CCC). The 'services' for users can be found on the internet at: www.copyright.com

For those organizations that have been granted a photocopy license, a separate system of payment has been arranged. Authorization does not extend to other kinds of copying, such as that for general distribution, for advertising or promotional purposes, for creating new collective works, or for resale. In the rest of the world: Permission to photocopy must be obtained from the copyright owner. Please apply to now Publishers Inc., PO Box 1024, Hanover, MA 02339, USA; Tel. +1 781 871 0245; www.nowpublishers.com; sales@nowpublishers.com

now Publishers Inc. has an exclusive license to publish this material worldwide. Permission to use this content must be obtained from the copyright license holder. Please apply to now Publishers, PO Box 179, 2600 AD Delft, The Netherlands, www.nowpublishers.com; e-mail: sales@nowpublishers.com

Annals of Corporate Governance
Volume 7, Issue 1, 2022
Editorial Board

Editors-in-Chief

Marc Goergen
IE Business School
Spain

Geoffrey Wood
Western University
Canada

Founding Editor

Douglas Cumming
Florida Atlantic University, USA

Senior Editors

Renee Adams
University of Oxford

Lucian Bebchuk
Harvard University

William Judge
Old Dominion University

Mark Roe
Harvard University

Rene Stulz
Ohio State University

James Westphal
University of Michigan

Editors

Amedeo de Cesari
Alliance Manchester Business School

Patricia Gabaldon
IE Business School

Aleksandra Gregoric
Copenhagen Business School

Anna Grosman
Loughborough University

Zulfiquer Haider
Western University

Hang Le
Nottingham Business School

Ben Sila
Edinburgh University Business School

Moshfique Uddin
Leeds University

Editorial Scope

Topics

Annals of Corporate Governance publishes articles in the following topics:

- Boards of Directors
- Ownership
- National Corporate Governance Mechanisms
- Comparative Corporate Governance Systems
- Self Governance
- Teaching Corporate Governance

Information for Librarians

Annals of Corporate Governance, 2022, Volume 7, 4 issues. ISSN paper version 2381-6724. ISSN online version 2381-6732. Also available as a combined paper and online subscription.

Contents

1 **Introduction**   3

2 **Digital Economies and the Case for Digital and Cybersecurity Governance**   7
    2.1 The Advancement of Digital Economies 8
    2.2 Defining and Calculating the Digital Economy 12
    2.3 The Digital Value Business Case for Corporate Boards . . . 14
    2.4 New Digital Worlds Bring New Risks 19

3 **Boardroom Mechanisms for Digital and Cybersecurity Governance**   25
    3.1 Digital and Cyber Governance Leading Practices 26
    3.2 Defining the Digitally Savvy Director 33
    3.3 The Technology and Cybersecurity Committee 35
    3.4 Calculating the Projected Economic Losses from Cyber Risk 37
    3.5 Governing Systemic Risk in Complex Digital Business Systems 39

4 **Self-Regulation: National Codes and Other Standards**   53
    4.1 Australia 55
    4.2 Japan 56

4.3	Malaysia	57
4.4	Nigeria	59
4.5	South Africa	61
4.6	The United States	65
4.7	International Organization for Standardization (ISO)	68
4.8	The DiRECTOR Framework for Systemic Risk Governance	71

5 Recommended Digital and Cybersecurity Governance Reforms — **73**

5.1	Digital Diversity Quotas and Digital Skills Disclosure	74
5.2	Board Structure and a Technology and Cybersecurity Committee	75
5.3	Cyber and Systemic Risk Disclosure	76

6 Conclusions — **79**

Appendix — **81**

References — **89**

Digital and Cybersecurity Governance Around the World

Bob Zukis

Founder and CEO, Digital Directors Network, and Adjunct Professor, USC Marshall School of Business, USA; bob@digitaldirectors.network

---

ABSTRACT

In countries around the world, economic dependency and growth is increasingly reliant upon the modern digital systems that power and enable services, products, and markets. Implementing and protecting these digital systems requires competent and capable public and private sector leadership actively governing the opportunities and risks of the digital future. While a small assortment of private sector corporate governance policies and practices exist worldwide related to digital and cybersecurity oversight, the broad-based application of structured boardroom oversight of these issues is both underdeveloped and underapplied and significantly lags the reality of how these technologies are impacting companies and societies in the modern world. This monograph coalesces some of the scattered but representative guidelines, rules and practices that are in existence in digital and risk governance. It also documents some of the recent developments in observed practices and regulatory rulemaking to develop a framework for digital and cybersecurity governance to develop this area as a necessary component of effective corporate governance worldwide.

Bob Zukis (2022), "Digital and Cybersecurity Governance Around the World", Annals of Corporate Governance: Vol. 7, No. 1, pp 1–92. DOI: 10.1561/109.00000032.
©2022 B. Zukis

1

Introduction

GDP and long-term business growth are increasingly dependent upon the complex digital systems that power and enable economies, companies, products, and services worldwide. Private enterprise is a leading part of the system that advances digital economies as businesses invest and innovate to adopt and apply Information and Communication Technologies (ICT) that create value for their investors and stakeholders.

However, many corporate boards are not actively or effectively governing digital and cyber risk as they struggle to understand and oversee the far-reaching implications of these technologies. Complex digital systems now support and directly power the operating systems that provide for many basic necessities in the modern world. The growing sophistication of cyber-attackers and their attacks threatens not just digital infrastructure, but the way of life for billions as the basic utilities that serve fundamental human needs and wants are also at risk because of digital risk.

Corporate governance practices and policies surrounding digital and cyber risk oversight are underdeveloped globally and where they do exist, they are sporadically adopted and applied. As the pace of digital change continues to accelerate, the reality of global corporate governance practices in digital and cyber risk oversight is that they significantly lag the dependencies we have upon digital technologies and their impacts. Corporate directors worldwide have statutory and fiduciary obligations to effectively govern their organizations and the implications of these issues. Not only does digital and cyber governance immaturity threaten the digital growth and progress that has been made to date, but it jeopardizes further advancements in realizing the full potential of the digital future.

COVID-19 and war in Ukraine have also served to expose, amplify, and reinforce some of the issues facing global boardrooms on digital and cybersecurity risk oversight. In a global survey of board governance issues during COVID-19, the Singapore Institute of Directors said (Marsh and McLennan, 2021):

> Digital readiness, or the lack of it, was exposed by the rapid shift to remote business operations. During the initial lockdown, many companies scrambled to ensure business continuity and workforce productivity under work-from-home conditions. While some boards oversaw the process of getting their companies to ramp up their digital capabilities and adapt to new business models, such as boosting online presence and exploring new markets, others decided to wait out the crisis, to their cost.

As the war against Ukraine continues, experts in cybersecurity warn that "...the potential remains for dramatic cyber attacks intended to demoralize Ukraine or countries supporting Ukraine" (Accenture, 2022).

Despite this challenging and changing cyber risk landscape, the benefits to humanity of digital technologies are becoming more apparent. While there are challenges in measuring the digital economy that include the existing conceptual boundaries of GDP, the prices of new and improved digital products, and unrecorded digital sector output (International Monetary Fund, 2018), the digital economy is already a significant direct and indirect contributor to global GDP. Analysts project that over 60% of global GDP is now digitized.

Consumers and citizens are experiencing digital transformation first-hand as the adoption of modern information and communication technologies like the smartphone have been far faster than prior advancements in similar consumer information technologies. Nevertheless, the early development of the digital economy has been uneven in emerging, developing, and developed economies worldwide. Other gaps in adoption and impact have been identified between men and women, private and public sectors, and urban and rural areas (UNCTAD, 2019).

The policies and programs that governments adopt to support and secure their ICT industry play a vital role in developing digital economies. Notwithstanding recent regulatory restraints imposed on their technology sector, China has demonstrated unprecedented momentum towards the digital future. Other countries, such as the United States, are facing risks that could slow down the progress that they have already made (Chakravorti *et al.*, 2020).

The adoption of these technologies by the companies operating within these countries has also been as uneven as many national efforts. Corporate progress even lags government responses in many respects. Regardless of the pace of change taking place in any company's journey to becoming a digital business, every boardroom still must understand and govern the digital and cybersecurity risks shaping the world around it. As the promise and potential of the digital future continue to work through its growing pains, its dangers are on full display. Attackers are freely exploiting weaknesses in digital systems and capitalizing on the far-reaching damages that they can inflict. Attackers are growing more sophisticated and include nation-states and well-organized, resourceful, and persistent amateur and professional groups. Industry reports pronounce that cybercrime will cost the global economy USD 10.5 trillion annually by 2025, making cybercrime the equivalent of the third-largest economy in the world, behind the U.S. and China (Morgan, 2020).

Cyber attackers are also exploiting systemic risk in new ways. Systemic risk is a dynamic new enterprise risk management challenge threatening every organization through its larger connected ecosystem. While some boardrooms are responding to these digitally driven and influenced challenges, many are not. As digital technologies and systems continue to transform economies and society, business dependence and reliance upon them will only continue to grow, as will their risks. Whether driven by a lack of understanding of the issues or uncertainty in how to respond, corporate governance is lagging in addressing these powerful forces of digital change.

Corporate governance policy and practice needs to rapidly advance to reflect the reality of the benefits and risks impacting humanity as a result of digital technologies. This monograph is intended to establish a baseline of the emerging issues and leading digital and cybersecurity governance practices to jumpstart this development. Documenting and aligning the current fragmentary nature of digital and cyber risk practices and policies worldwide can help bring clarity to this emerging area of corporate governance. It will help establish a foundation which can then be built upon by policymakers and boardrooms to govern their economies and businesses safely and securely into the digital future.

This monograph starts by analyzing some of the work being done to study and isolate the digital aspect of economies to illustrate what is at stake. Various existing boardroom practices and policies in digital and cyber risk oversight are then identified to bring some transparency to the work already being done to improve how corporate boards govern these issues. Select national codes and standards from a diverse group of countries is then highlighted together with emerging regulatory trends to illustrate the widely acknowledged nature of this problem from practitioners and regulators.

It is intended that this monograph contributes to a structured approach to understanding these issues to create a framework for more specific solutions that can be broadly implemented to advance digital and cyber risk governance.

2

Digital Economies and the Case for Digital and Cybersecurity Governance

Understanding the importance of effective digital and cyber risk corporate governance policies and practices requires an appreciation for the importance of these tools. While their impacts span social, political, legal, ethical and demographic realms, it is their economic impacts that are often the center of attention in the corporate boardroom.

Computers have been described as the general-purpose technology (GPT) of our era (Brynjolfsson and McAfee, 2011). Like the general-purpose technologies of electricity, steam power, and the internal combustion engine, these technological innovations are described as "so powerful that they interrupt and accelerate the normal march of economic progress" (Brynjolfsson and McAfee (2011), p. 20). Computers and ICT systems are creating complex and powerful new information systems that are core to business value propositions and economic growth.

Information systems are not new, although their levels of connectivity and much of the data now being gathered by them is. The printing press can lay claim to the first technology that enabled an information system at scale. The landline telephone was, and remains for some, a distant relative to the information systems being enabled by today's

ICT technologies. Information systems have long been the backbone of corporations and economic growth. Cities that adopted the information system of the printing press demonstrated economic growth rates 385% greater than the cities that did not (Dittmar, 2011). The vast amounts of digital data that is now collected, analyzed, and used through today's information systems constantly expands the frontiers of innovation and risk related to these tools and our dependence upon them throughout the modern world.

The business and personal value enabled by today's many digital products and services is on full display as the world responded to COVID-19. As work from home became a necessity and requirement, digital business systems allowed employees to stay connected with each other and with their customers and suppliers. Digital business systems also allowed corporate directors to continue to do their job as board meetings moved online. These technologies helped people socialize, shop, learn and be entertained during this unprecedented time. Never before has the value of connectivity and these digital technologies been this tested, or this validated.

2.1 The Advancement of Digital Economies

As economies and companies worldwide have adopted ICT tools and technologies, they have invested heavily and innovated to digitally transform their economies and businesses. These public and private sector initiatives require effective governance to thrive and remain sustainable. Old models of governance and approaches need to be rethought to be relevant to the new challenges and risks that digital economies and businesses present.

The direct and indirect impacts of these digital transformations can be seen by looking at changes in the list of the ten most valuable companies in the world over the last two decades. Only Bank of America remains on the 2021 Forbes list of the ten largest public companies from their first list in 2003 (Haverstock, 2021). Forbes equally weights assets, market value, sales, and profits in coming up with their list (Table 2.1).

2.1. The Advancement of Digital Economies

Singapore, Hong Kong, the United States, South Korea, Lithuania, and several others. Singapore tops their numerical rankings on digital stock. The United States has lower momentum rates than others, reflecting challenges with cybersecurity, misinformation, disinformation, and technology industry trust.

The *Break Outs* have less of a digital base but are catching up fast and include China, Azerbaijan, Russia, India, Iran, and Vietnam. China is noteworthy as a significant positive outlier in its momentum towards the digital future. This analysis was completed before the technology sector government interventions that are now negatively impacting the equity values of some of China's technology leaders. Notwithstanding the current regulatory focus on some of China's technology leaders, China's digital might, momentum, and global economic influence will continue to affect the world's digitally influenced future.

Vietnam's Prime Minister has announced a national digital transformation initiative with a goal for Vietnam's digital economy to be 20% of GDP by 2025 and 30% by 2030 (Lee, 2021). Keys to their plan include recognizing that institutions are the driving force of digital transformation, and that safety and network security are critical to sustainability. Notably, they explicitly call out the essential role of leadership in achieving this vision, recognizing that the heads of agencies, organizations, and enterprises must be committed and promote the development of the digital future.

The *Stall Outs* they identified have a high level of digital maturity but are showing signs of slowing and include Denmark, New Zealand, Japan, France, and Australia. Furthermore, the countries they categorize as *Watch Outs* have a low digital base and a lack of momentum towards a digital future. These countries face challenges on both dimensions and include South Africa, Italy, Turkey, Ecuador, and Egypt.

Notably, even though South Africa is categorized as facing some significant challenges as a digital economy, their IT governance policies are a pioneer and leader in corporate governance policies worldwide. The *King IV Report* from the Institute of Directors in Southern Africa provides one of the most comprehensive national corporate governance standards that integrates comprehensive principles and recommendations for digital governance. *King IV* is discussed in further detail in

Section 4.5. South Africa however faces other systemic weaknesses in the private and public systems needed to enable digital economies which are working against the overall progress that country is making towards being a digital economy. This reinforces the importance and criticality of there being a high-performing public and private system in place working together towards the digital future. Weakness in one area of the overall system including governance, management, regulation or lack of a coordinated public-private approach can significantly impair the digital ambitions of any economy or business.

Economies worldwide need a well-functioning system in place in order for a digital economy to emerge and thrive, including the role that private enterprise plays within the larger system. Digital businesses also need a well-functioning digital system to thrive. One that includes a digitally competent and effective corporate boardroom. Private enterprises and their corporate boardrooms are critical parts of every country's far reaching ambitions to provide a digitally competitive and secure environment for their citizens.

2.2 Defining and Calculating the Digital Economy

There is not yet a commonly accepted definition of the digital economy. However, it is generally recognized to include firms who are in the digital sector, i.e., the producers and servicers of digital tools and technologies, those building digitally native products and services on this foundation, and the non-digitally native firms and organizations who are adopting these tools and technologies to transform their businesses, products, and services.

The United Nations offers a layered definition of the digital economy that progressively broadens to reflect the expanding adoption of ICT and the digitalization of different non-digitally native sectors. The first level of their digital economy definition spans the core producers of foundational ICT technologies. These firms produce semiconductors, processors, computers, and telecommunication devices that power the enabling foundations of the digital economy, i.e., the internet and telecom infrastructures. The next level is the digital and information technology sectors that build products and solutions upon this foundation. The last

2.2. Defining and Calculating the Digital Economy

level represents other sectors that are adopting digital and information technologies to transform themselves. The last layer presents the most significant challenges towards measuring and quantifying the digital economy (UNCTAD, 2019).

Industry analysts estimate that 65% of global GDP will be digitized by 2022 (IDC, 2020). In 2019 the World Economic Forum declared that 60% of global GDP would be digitized by 2022, contrasted by the statement that only 45% of people trust that technology will improve their lives (World Economic Forum, 2019). These estimates significantly exceed estimates from 2017 that projected the digital economy to reach almost 25% of global GDP by 2025 (Huawei and Oxford Economics, 2017). Current estimates reflect improvements in our understanding of the breadth and depth of the digital economy, along with our ability to understand and measure its expanding spillover or indirect benefits. These indirect benefits are estimated to outweigh their direct benefits by a ratio of 3:1. Moreover, over the last three decades, it is estimated that 20 US dollars has been added to GDP for every one US dollar invested in digital technologies. A rate of economic impact 6.7 times the rate for non-digital investments (Huawei and Oxford Economics, 2017).

Artificial intelligence and machine learning developments are estimated to add USD 13 trillion to annual global economic output by 2030 (International Telecommunication Union, 2018). Other digitally native and influenced technologies, including cloud computing, the internet of things, 5G, robotics, and blockchain, will also continue to have widespread business, social, legal, political, and economic impacts along with the disruptions and transformations that they bring and influence.

Governments are also working on estimating the scale and impact of the digital economy on their GDP calculations. The U.S. Bureau of Economic Analysis has been working to broaden its definition of the digital economy to begin to accommodate goods and services that are partially digital, in addition to those that are primarily digital. This broadened definition of the U.S. digital economy reflects infrastructure, e-commerce, and priced digital services where a fee is charged to the consumer for computing and communication. The U.S. government estimated that in 2019 the U.S. digital economy represented 9.6% (USD 2.051 trillion) of the U.S. current-dollar gross domestic product of USD

21.433 trillion. It trails only real estate and rental and leasing (13.4%), government (12.3%), and manufacturing (10.9%) sectors in the share of total U.S. gross domestic product (U.S. Bureau of Economic Analysis, 2021). Notably, from 2005–2019 the U.S. government estimates that the U.S. digital economy's real value-added grew at an average annual rate of 6.5% compared with 1.8% for the total U.S. economy (p. 2).

While measuring a digital economy has some challenges, growth in the digital economy far exceeds growth in the non-digital sector. As the spillover economic effects as these technologies become more widely distributed beyond the core ICT industry, digital growth and digitally influenced growth will continue to expand. Gaps could also widen between the digital haves and have nots at the country, company and individual levels.

While the impressive growth rates of the digital economy are expected to continue, they are not guaranteed as significant risks are mounting. Cybersecurity, misinformation, disinformation, and a growing level of digital distrust threaten the advancement and future of digital economies and businesses worldwide. As the economic benefits of digital technologies spill over into the general economy, their risks do as well. The 2021 ransomware attack on Colonial Pipeline in the United States shut down America's largest energy pipeline, creating widespread disruption into the general economy. Other cyber-generated threats and risks to critical infrastructure are also expanding globally. Attackers are also pivoting their attack strategy and tactics, recognizing that the damage they can inflict is not limited to digital infrastructure but to the ability of a company or organization to function. These spillover risks are threatening the very foundation of businesses and economies. Cybersecurity is not just about protecting digital assets and infrastructure; it is now about protecting business, economic, social, and national interests.

2.3 The Digital Value Business Case for Corporate Boards

Every nation needs to actively govern its migration to the digital future. Corporate boards also have a duty to actively govern these issues. Every company is directly and indirectly influenced by the

18.4% of advanced economy GDP in 2017, while it accounted for only 10% of GDP in developing economies. These estimates peg the global digital economy in 2017 at USD 11.5 trillion, or 15.5% of global GDP. The expected growth rate of the world's digital economy at that time was projected to be 2.5 times the rate of global GDP growth over the next 15-years (Huawei and Oxford Economics, 2017).

Projections and estimates of the growth of the digital economy highlight the significant influence that modern digital technologies have on economies. Each country's economic evolution into a digital economy depends on a coordinated and complementary system of public and private sector governance, leadership, investment, and innovation.

The *Digital Intelligence Index* developed by The Fletcher School at Tufts University tracks 358 indicators across 90 economies to produce a *Digital Evolution* scorecard and *Digital Trust* scorecard. The *Digital Intelligence Index* provides a comprehensive country level analysis of its state and rate of digital evolution. Their analysis segments 90 countries into four groups — *Stand Outs, Stall Outs, Break Outs*, and *Watch Outs* (see Figure A.1). These groupings categorize different national levels of digital maturity alongside the momentum towards each country's digital future, representing an analysis of nation-state digital stock and flow.

In assessing the state and momentum of these digital economies, digital indicators are grouped into four categories: country-level supply conditions, demand conditions, the institutional environment, innovation, and change. Supply conditions at the national level consider how well developed the digital backbone and infrastructure is within the country that enables digital interactions and transactions. Demand conditions consider how willing and able consumers are to engage with the country's digital ecosystem. Government investment, policy, and regulation also play a crucial role in creating a high-performing institutional environment with beneficial laws and regulations that facilitate stability, trust, and further investment in time and resources by consumers and companies. Finally, a system that fuels digital innovation and changes, from talent to capital and R&D, is also required.

The *Stand Outs* reflect mature digital economies with indications that suggest positive momentum towards the digital future and include

2.1. The Advancement of Digital Economies

Table 2.1: The world's most valuable public companies

2003	2021
1 Citigroup	1 Industrial and Commercial Bank of China
2 General Electric	2 JPMorgan Chase & Co
3 American International Group	3 Berkshire Hathaway
4 ExxonMobil	4 China Construction Bank
5 Bank of America	5 Saudi Arabian Oil Company
6 Royal Dutch/Shell Group	6 Apple
7 British Petroleum	7 Bank of America
8 Fannie Mae	8 Ping An Insurance Company of China
9 HRBC Group	9 Agricultural Bank of China
10 Toyota Motor	10 Amazon.com

Apple and Amazon have now made the 2021 list displacing oil & gas behemoth Royal Dutch/Shell Group and Japanese automobile company Toyota.

The 2021 list also has heavy representation from Chinese companies. China and the United States are the world's two leading digital economies with 50% of global spending on the internet of things, more than 75% of the cloud computing market, and 90% of the market capitalization of the world's 70 largest digital platforms (UNCTAD, 2019).

Digital technologies have helped reshape the global corporate landscape in less than two decades. This new corporate world order and the influence that these digital leaders and digitally influenced businesses have in their countries and worldwide will continue to drive digitally infused change and disruption that impacts humanity, businesses, and economies worldwide.

As global corporate leadership has shifted over the last two decades, digital economies have evolved as well. However, digital economies are not equally developed worldwide. Vast differences exist in digital maturity between nation-states as the growth and impact of digital economies are being enabled and experienced differently in emerging, developing, and developed economies. While measuring the digital economy remains a challenge, some measures indicate the digital economy accounted for

2.3. The Digital Value Business Case for Corporate Boards

strategic and operational influences and implications of the evolution of digital economies. Each company's digital success is also critically dependent upon the system it creates for its own digital evolution. And the corporate boardroom is a critical control point within that corporate system — a control point that needs to effectively govern the digital upside and its downside implications.

The business impacts of having a digitally savvy board have been determined to be significant for U.S. listed companies. MIT's Center for Information Systems Research identified the financial performance impacts for companies with "digitally savvy" boardrooms in 2019. These benefits included 38 percent higher revenue growth over three years, 34 percent higher growth in return on assets, 34 percent higher market capitalization growth, and 17 percent higher profit margins. These results were observed where the board had a critical mass of at least three digitally savvy corporate directors — an observation in only 24 percent of U.S. listed companies with revenue over $1 billion (Weill et al., 2019).

As digital technologies and their impacts on economies develop worldwide, corporate boards, their abilities, and the approaches they take to govern the implications of these issues must advance alongside these market forces. Rodney Adkins, who sits on multiple U.S. public company corporate boards puts it this way, "Boardroom skills need to reflect the patterns of the marketplace" (Zukis, 2022).

The boardroom challenge is not just limited to governing cybersecurity. It is also about understanding and governing the opportunities that digital technologies present to create value, establish competitive advantage, and solve problems that impact the long-term sustainability of the firm and the many stakeholders that rely upon it.

While the general business value drivers of revenue growth, profitability, and market capitalization are universal measures in for-profit organizations, digital platforms and ICT technologies can create and deliver value in new ways for different stakeholders. Corporate boards and directors have a responsibility to understand and actively govern how digital technologies are creating, redefining, and delivering new sources of business value.

New digital technologies are capturing and enabling new forces that can be exploited in new ways. With the widespread consumer adoption of ICT's like smartphones, businesses have now bridged the last-mile and last-minute of connectivity with their stakeholders and markets. Understanding and bridging spatial and temporal relevance is shifting value propositions and allowing new markets to be created and inefficient ones to be reached. Breaching spatial and temporal boundaries with these tools shifts and impacts the foundational parts of many businesses' value propositions. Control over these new forces causes the associations between activity, time, and place to splinter. As a result, activities fragment (Bayarma *et al.*, 2011). This is moving the post-industrial information society to one that is person-focused, not place-focused.

During COVID-19, the advent of large-scale work from home practices is an example of this occurring at scale. While forced by COVID-19, this shift redefined the relationship between work, the office, and the organization and was only made possible by the use of digital technologies. Questions such as how cities will be impacted along with the many systems that have been built to aggregate workers in city centers still need to be answered. Others such as whether people will begin to spread out and move to rural environments when they no longer need to congregate in a central office environment together with the environmental, political, economic, and social impact of this kind of migration need to be studied. Many other issues such as the impacts on traffic patterns, public transportation, support services, housing, and the tax base are all unanswered and facing the potential of foundational shifts.

Apple's watch has now delivered some essential medical monitoring functions to the wearer's wrist in real-time with the ability to monitor blood oxygen levels, heart rate, and heart rhythm with electrocardiogram (ECG) functionality. How does this shift change the nature and services performed within a hospital, such as its staffing requirements and facility design when these functions no longer need to be performed onsite? How will healthcare monitoring, diagnosis, and treatment shift when these functions can be monitored in real-time, in the context of a unique activity directly from the wearer's wrist?

Some businesses are only possible because of the new information systems that can be built from these new technologies. Uber's entire business model is only possible because of its ability to make a market by harnessing location-specific information in real-time between those needing transportation and those willing to provide it.

Amazon and Alibaba's secret sauce is their ability to reduce transaction costs significantly to make highly efficient online markets. The concept of transaction costs is fundamental to making a market, and every company is in the business of making markets. Amazon's e-commerce platform is the foundation of the company and is one of the most efficient markets in the world.

In an interview with the Dean of the Fletcher School of Business at Tufts University, he said, "There is much more happening beneath the technology than what we realize, and we need to be paying attention to the details. It is not the big advancements around hardware and software. It is the invisible creep and smaller changes that are changing things" (Zukis, 2021a).

Creating value is what powers every business. Capturing it is what defines financial success or failure. Business has always been about innovation — a way to organize and reward human activity for creating value by solving humanity's problems. However, value can be a fluid and transient concept. It can be individually unique, influenceable, and not easy to predict. Value is derived from connectivity, price, access, vanity, shelter, entertainment, discovery, time, knowledge, choice, security, health, access, social benefit, useability, reliability, privacy, convenience, comfort, rarity, longevity, ego, trust, quality, self-esteem, simplicity, and many other qualities. What is valued comes in many shapes, sizes, and forms. How these needs, wants, and problems are fulfilled form the foundations of every company's value proposition. Whether a product or service is embedded with intrinsic or perceived worth, people value different things for different reasons, at different times and in different circumstances.

Digital technologies redefine these value propositions and provide new tools that solve problems that can create and deliver value in new ways. In addition to exploiting new forces like spatial and temporal relevance, digital value is derived from the two macro issues of digital data and platformization (UNCTAD, 2019). Digital technologies bring new abilities to gather, collect, monitor, analyze, and learn from previously unavailable data. New types of data are also being gathered at a scale never before possible. The information systems built from this data can identify, add, create and capture value in new ways from every part of a business value chain.

Information systems that convert this data into information, knowledge, and action can help companies improve operations, act faster and more efficiently, understand markets better, make better decisions, create new products and services, reach new markets, make markets more efficient, develop new business models, partner differently, improve employee productivity and compete in new ways.

Embedding digital technologies in non-digital products or services also creates new products and businesses that change the value proposition, risks, and business models of companies. Hasbro, a U.S. public company famous for toys and games such as Mr. Potato Head, Play-Doh, Monopoly, Transformers, and many other childhood staples, is evolving into a highly driven and dependent digital technology company. In 2020 Hasbro derived more than USD 1 billion from e-commerce revenues, a 43% increase from 2019. Of this, the e-commerce channel of Amazon.com accounted for 10% of their 2020 revenue. They also disclosed in their regulatory disclosures "rapid technological change" as a threat to their business along with "increasing competition with technology companies" together with their ability to grow their digital gaming business as keys to their future success (Hasbro, Inc., 2020). Hasbro's corporate board is playing a lead role in this digital transformation through digital and cyber competent directors on their board and a focused data privacy and cyber boardroom committee.

Walmart, one of the largest companies in the world, is entering the enterprise software industry. They have announced that they will sell the retail technologies they have built and use internally to other companies (Perez, 2021). Walmart's board has long been an innovator in digital governance. They introduced a technology and e-commerce committee onto their board in 2011 to govern the strategic digital issues facing Walmart due to the competitive threat of Amazon. They have corporate directors on this committee with deep and broad digital domain expertise. Selling enterprise software introduces a significant business model change for Walmart that will also introduce new risks to them, their software customers, their existing customers, their investors, and other stakeholders. Effectively governing these issues has been, and remains a core priority and responsibility of the Walmart board.

"Platformization" is also a foundational digital value proposition behind digital transformation. Platformization is nothing more than a concept that reflects the ability of digital technologies to create efficient and new marketplaces. Digital platforms connect large extended ecosystems efficiently, i.e., buyers, sellers, suppliers, communities, and partners. Every company is in the business of making a market, and digital technologies are changing how markets can be created and reached. Digital technologies can extend and reach the "long-tail" of an inefficient market through these technologies. Uber, Airbnb, Etsy, and many other companies have created new markets that would not have been possible without today's digital technologies.

As more economic growth and value is derived, influenced, and delivered by digital technologies, corporate boards have no choice but to govern these new opportunities and their risks.

2.4 New Digital Worlds Bring New Risks

In addition to governing the strategic impact of digital technologies and how they create value, corporate boards are responsible for protecting the value that their organizations create and capture. New digital technologies and the many innovations they deliver, have introduced new and complex risks.

The equity risks of significant data breaches are well documented both in the short and long term. In 2017, Equifax's stock price dropped to USD 92.80 from USD 141.59 in two weeks as a result of their well-publicized breach. Analysis of data breaches concludes that a short-term negative impact of the breach on a company's equity value is common. However, long-term impacts on equity value are inconclusive, with some differences in impact identified by the organizations sector. Contributors to long-term negative impacts include companies in the financial sector, the type of information breached, and the firm's size as cyber impacts can be much more punitive and even create existential risks for smaller firms (Huang *et al.*, 2019).

Notwithstanding equity risk and impact, the real economic impacts of cyber risk can be material and are rising, as are their litigation costs and implications. The economic impacts of cyber risk include the costs of responding to a breach, fines, business interruptions, the cost of ransomware, and the misappropriation of assets, both tangible and intangible. Over the last five years, the top 5 data loss events have had actual financial impacts exceeding one billion US dollars, almost equaling 50% of annual revenue for the companies impacted in two of these five cases (Cyentia Institute LLC, 2020).

Significant data breaches where the exposed data records exceed 50 million records have a cost multiplier of 100× as compared to the average global data breach and cost on average USD 401 million. The average cost of a data breach increased by almost 10 percent between 2020 and 2021 (IBM Security, 2021). Actual costs are also increasing for ransomware payments and their related business continuity impacts as attackers increase their focus on extortion and the power of ransomware to significantly impair an organizations ability to function.

Ransomware is now the fastest-growing cybersecurity threat because it works to inflict the most damage and this gets attackers paid. Ransomware is such a growing problem that it is a top priority for the Biden administration in the United States, which has said, "The number and size of ransomware incidents have increased significantly and strengthening our nation's resilience from cyberattacks – both private and public sector – is a top priority of the President's" (Neuberger, 2021).

In a major initiative, Australia's government is asking for public opinion on establishing a new standard to address cybersecurity risk and the AUD 3.5 billion a year that cyber-crime is costing the Australian economy (Commonwealth of Australia, 2021). Australia's Minister for Home Affairs, Karen Andrews, has warned that corporate directors could potentially be held personally liable if their companies suffer a cyber-attack as a way to get cybersecurity risk under control (Galloway, 2021).

2.4. New Digital Worlds Bring New Risks

Japan is updating its cybersecurity strategy from 2018. It will continue to abide by five fundamental principles, including assurance of the free flow of information, the rule of law, openness, autonomy, and collaboration among multi-stakeholders. Key policy initiatives of the Japanese national strategy include raising executive awareness around digitalization and cybersecurity and promoting more effective practices around ascertaining risk and disclosing corporate information (National Center for Incident Readiness and Strategy for Cybersecurity, 2021).

India is also releasing an updated national cybersecurity strategy. Reports indicate that the new strategy will encompass around 80 key deliverables, including data as a critical national resource and the need for cyber auditing (The Hindu, 2021). India's Ministry of Electronics and Information Technology has implemented a six-hour cyber incident disclosure rule that goes into effect in July 2022 for critical parts of India's network and IT infrastructure industry, and explained this requirement this way "Reporting incidents can lead to sharing of information, preventing the risk of systemic risks and leading to a stronger ecosystem" (Pritchard, 2022).

In December 2020, the EU released their *Cybersecurity Strategy for the Digital Decade* in response to the growing number of cyber-attacks. Recognizing the growing cyber threats to the general economy, they refer to the fact that there were over 450 cybersecurity incidents in 2019 involving critical European infrastructure. Focused on regulatory, investment, and various policy initiatives, EU actions over the next decade in cybersecurity will be focused on (European Commission, 2020):

- Resilience, technology sovereignty, and leadership;
- Building operational capacity to prevent, deter and respond; and
- Advancing a global and open cyberspace.

While there are not yet explicit indications of corporate governance reform related to digital and cyber risk in the initiative, the implications of this strategy will impact EU companies and require active boardroom leadership to understand how organizations will be impacted by it. As nation-states ramp up governance around the security of their ICT industry and infrastructures, boardrooms need to do the same as the nature of digital risk is changing and creating far-reaching business, litigation, and equity risks.

When U.S. Federal Reserve Chairman Jerome Powell was asked during a television interview in 2021 about the chances of another systemic breakdown like the one that occurred during 2008 in the financial sector, he said that the chances of that happening were "... very, very low." He then went on to say, "But the world changes. The world evolves. And the risks change as well. And I would say that the risk we keep our eyes on the most now is cyber risk" (Powell, 2021).

The U.S. Securities and Exchange Commission (SEC) has now proposed transformational rule changes that would introduce corporate governance transformation and new levels of boardroom accountability on cybersecurity. This includes requiring director cyber expertise disclosure and a new incident disclosure trigger that would put the burden on issuers to understand materiality in the context of cyber risk (Zukis, 2022). These proposed requirements could act as a global catalyst for how corporate boards govern cyber risk. Much in the same way that the Sarbanes-Oxley Act of 2002 not only transformed U.S. corporate governance, but influenced and advanced corporate governance practices worldwide around financial reporting and integrity.

Over the last several decades, the incredible advancement and adoption of information and communication technologies have enabled humanity to create many innovations and different ways of supporting the needs and wants of almost 8 billion people. Many of the systems that have been built are powered by an expanding group of new information-powered technologies that have solved old problems, met new needs, but introduced new risks. Because of these technologies, social, economic, environmental, political, legal, and ethical norms and boundaries have been challenged, breached, and redefined. During 2020, the shared global experience of COVID-19 demonstrated the utility and power of these technologies by keeping people and organizations working, learning, dining, shopping, and engaged with one another. COVID-19 shut down location-based physical in-person engagement, but the digital economy kept things running for the digitally enabled. These technologies also

2.4. New Digital Worlds Bring New Risks

introduced strategic and competitive risks for companies and boards that lagged in understanding their value propositions. For everyone, these technologies introduced a vast collection of new and evolving risks, including existential ones.

The New York Times reported that a ransomware attack on a hospital's computers delayed medical treatment in Germany, causing a fatality (Eddy and Perlroth, 2020). Travelex, a company with over 1,000 employees, was reported to be forced into bankruptcy because of a ransomware attack in 2020 (BNP Media, 2020). Described as the "largest attack on the U.S. energy system in history" (Bordoff, 2021), the Colonial Pipeline ransomware attack in 2021 and the subsequent shutdown of their energy pipeline on the east coast of the United States not only disrupted the energy market but impacted millions of consumers and businesses.

The complex, deeply inter-connected digital systems that are being built are themselves fraught with inherent risks. However, they have also introduced a much broader collection of extended risks to create new dimensions of systemic risk never before present throughout society. A growing body of boardroom policies and practices is emerging to govern these issues.

3

Boardroom Mechanisms for Digital and Cybersecurity Governance

The purpose of corporate governance is described by the OECD to "...help build an environment of trust, transparency and accountability necessary for fostering long-term investment, financial stability and business integrity, thereby supporting stronger growth and more inclusive societies" (OECD, 2015).

As digital technologies permeate the world, this makes them a core part of the corporate governance remit. Corporate directors worldwide share a responsibility to "...balance the interests of the company, shareholders, and other stakeholders by ensuring long-term growth that is sustainable and profitable" (SpencerStuart, 2017, p. 10).

In a global survey of corporate directors focusing on Asia Pacific, 82 percent of the director respondents believe the boardroom, not IT departments, should lead digital transformation efforts (Tricor Group and FT Board Director Programme, 2021). A senior leader at the U.S. Federal Trade Commission, which protects America's consumers stated that "Contrary to popular belief, data security begins with the board of directors, not the IT department" (Ho, 2021).

Corporate boards and directors have a clear responsibility to govern the value creating opportunities of these tools, and their risks. Board reform and development on any issue comes through "hard" reforms driven by law and regulations and "soft" advancements driven by leading practices and learned effectiveness.

The adaptability of boardroom policy and practice to change is an inherent concept in corporate governance but not an intrinsic practice in many boardrooms. The OECD's guiding principles for public company corporate governance reflect the need for boards to be as adaptable and agile as the companies they govern. OECD's principles-based framework for corporate governance states that this is foundationally an issue of competitive advantage, "To remain competitive in a changing world, corporations must innovate and adapt their corporate governance practices so that they can meet new demands and grasp new opportunities" (OECD, 2015, p. 11). A body of leading practices along with legislative reforms is emerging that can form a foundation in digital and cyber risk oversight that can be distributed and built upon.

3.1 Digital and Cyber Governance Leading Practices

Over the last several decades, there has been a proliferation of guidance, codes, frameworks, opinions, ratings, and benchmarks as corporate governance has matured as a practice and profession worldwide. General corporate boardroom practices have now reached a stage of maturity where what corporate boards do and how they do it is a topic of evaluation and ratings that factor into equity investment and risk.

Corporate governance evaluation serves multiple purposes, including the needs of individual and institutional investors to assess and monitor the specific corporate governance practices that may impact how corporations allocate their resources and predict the performance of their investments. A heightened global focus and ongoing debate on the corporation's purpose also focuses attention on corporate governance and motivates shareholder and stakeholder activism that demands transparency and accountability from the boardroom and corporate directors. Corporate boards and their directors apply a wide range of rules, practices, policies, and tactics in the performance of their overall duties. Whether shaped by law or regulation, leading or emerging practice, or local cultural influence, corporate governance practices differ worldwide

3.1. Digital and Cyber Governance Leading Practices

across boardrooms, and they have evolved over time. While many of these practices are unique to individual boardrooms and jurisdictions, there is a strong unilateral common foundation behind the principles and objectives of corporate governance.

Most corporate boards apply a hybrid approach that follows legal or regulatory mandates such as corporate law, listing requirements, or other national and local laws or regulations together with voluntary or self-regulated practices and policies applied from national codes and leading practices. The amount of structured guidance in digital and cybersecurity oversight is less voluminous than in many other areas of corporate governance, the problem this monograph is designed to address.

Cyber risk is emerging as a factor of ESG analysis (International Organization Of Securities Commissions, 2021). Environmental, social, and governance (ESG) data, ratings, and investment analysis has rapidly emerged with a heavy focus on environmental and social issues. Institutional Shareholder Services (ISS), a global leader in evaluating general corporate governance practices, tracks and evaluates over 230 factors for 6,000 companies in 30 markets worldwide in coming up with their Governance QualityScore (ISS, 2021). ISS segments their 230+ general corporate governance factors into four foundational categories when grading corporate governance: board structure, compensation, shareholder rights, and audit and risk oversight.

Leading practices in board structure and risk oversight are starting to emerge on digital and cyber governance. While the pace of legal and regulatory reform on digital and cybersecurity governance is slow, legal and regulatory reform on data privacy and cybersecurity management has been very robust in response to the significant data breaches of Equifax, Target and many others around the world. A crisis in cybersecurity is not an exaggeration as regulators realize these issues are squarely in the interest of investors, consumers, and citizens. Regulators have been enforcing the many rules that they have legislated through significant penalties and fines, and often with concomitant corporate governance reforms to go along with these ex-post actions.

Forced regulatory action resulting from crisis situations has driven rapid boardroom reform in the past, as it did in the United States with the federal law known as the Sarbanes-Oxley Act of 2002 (SOX). The enactment of SOX in the United States cascaded and created similar governance reforms around the world. SOX drove boardroom reform on director independence, committee structure, disclosure, and board composition, among other reforms. On board composition, it established a mandate for U.S. public companies to include financially literate directors on audit committees. At least one of these committee members needs to be disclosed as a financial expert under SOX.

SOX was a boardroom "sledgehammer" born of the existential threat that U.S. capital markets faced regarding the loss of investor confidence in financial reporting brought about by Enron and the other financial reporting scandals of the time. The scale and speed of the corporate governance reforms enacted by SOX were an exception in the history of boardroom reform.

Regulators in some markets, notably the United States, are effective in acting as ex-post cybersecurity governance regulators imposing new cyber risk governance requirements to the companies that they impose penalties and fines upon. The unprecedented USD 5 billion U.S. Federal Trade Commission (FTC) fine of Facebook for data privacy violations requires Facebook to adopt specific corporate governance reforms, including adopting an independent privacy committee on their board. The FTC order also forces greater management accountability on data privacy and data security by requiring Facebook to add privacy officers who report to the board committee with quarterly sign offs. CEO Mark Zuckerberg must also sign off on Facebook's compliance with the order's mandated data privacy program and false certifications carry civil and criminal penalties. Third-party verification of Facebook's compliance with the mandated data privacy program is also required every two years (Federal Trade Commission, 2019).

However in digital and cybersecurity risk oversight, worldwide regulatory and legal regimes have not yet forced significant preventative digital governance reforms. This is in contrast to the number of new laws and regulations on cybersecurity and data privacy that organizations are already being forced to comply with. This is changing, and the SEC may lead the way again in global corporate governance reform—however this time it is with regard to cyber governance.

3.1. Digital and Cyber Governance Leading Practices

Following a similar approach to the one taken with SOX, the SEC has proposed new rules that will force cyber governance transformation into America's public company corporate boardrooms (U.S. Securities and Exchange Commission, 2022b). Two particular areas of their proposed rules will significantly transform how America's corporate boards govern cyber risk.

First, a proposed rule would expressly require U.S. registrants to disclose information about a cybersecurity incident within four business days after the registrant determines that it has experienced a material cybersecurity incident, as opposed to the incident's date of discovery.

The SEC is also proposing disclosures need to be more prescriptive in describing the incident, including:

- When the incident was discovered and whether it is ongoing;
- A brief description of the nature and scope of the incident;
- Whether any data was stolen, altered, accessed, or used for any other unauthorized purpose;
- The effect of the incident on the registrant's operations; and
- Whether the registrant has remediated or is currently remediating the incident.

The proposed rules note, "We believe that this information would provide timely and relevant disclosure to investors and other market participants (such as financial analysts, investment advisers, and portfolio managers) and enable them to assess the possible effects of a material cybersecurity incident on the registrant, including any long-term and short-term financial effects or operational effects."

Notably, this change includes a subtle yet impactful shift to when an incident should be reported. The proposed rules require disclosure "within four business days after the registrant determines that it has experienced a material cybersecurity incident." The prior "general" standard was the date that an incident was discovered. This new disclosure trigger date puts a significant and increased burden on issuers to understand the impacts of a cyber breach and what constitutes materiality in the eyes of a reasonable investor.

As ransomware continues to escalate, the business impacts of cyber risk are now extending well beyond equity risk. They include significant financial costs, fines, penalties and litigation costs, business continuity risks, and the far-reaching economic exposures of third-party and other systemic risk impacts. This new proposed provision will not only require companies to understand materiality in the context of a breach, but it will have the effect of challenging boards and management teams to understand their cyber risk environment more fully in financial terms before breaches occur.

Calculating projected or expected cyber losses in economic terms is something rarely observed at present. But estimating this potential liability shares common ground with any estimate of probable and estimable losses such as loan loss reserves for banks, warranty liabilities for manufacturers or doubtful accounts receivable for any company. Whereas corporate boards and leadership may have felt that cyber insurance effectively transferred the majority of their cyber risk exposure to a third-party, the reality of the expanding impacts of cyber risk means that issuers are primarily self-insured for the significant majority of the cyber risks and costs that they face. This proposed change will now force corporate boards and management to have a new understanding of the far-reaching economic impacts inherent within their cyber risk environment, the effectiveness of their cyber control practices and policies, and the specific economic impacts of a breach.

Early in 2022, it was reported that both Bridgestone (Greig, 2022) and Toyota (Hawkins, 2022) shut down parts of their factory operations because of a cyber-attack. Not as a direct result of the attack, but because they apparently did not understand how cyber risk impacts their boarder operating environment. Presumably, this was the only way they could control the impacts of the breaches. Forcing U.S. issuers to understand materiality is a subtle but powerful proposed SEC rule which would force boards and management teams to have a much greater depth of understanding of the potential and specific business impacts of cyber risk.

The second proposed SEC rule would require corporate boards to disclose if a corporate director has cyber expertise. One of the sweeping changes made by The Sarbanes-Oxley Act of 2002 was for

3.1. Digital and Cyber Governance Leading Practices

issuers to disclose if they had a qualified financial expert amongst their corporate director ranks (Zukis, 2016). An obvious boardroom competency in hindsight, the SEC's new proposed rule is now addressing director competencies on cybersecurity. Strengthening the boardroom as a critical cyber control function in 2022 is as vital as strengthening the boardroom as a critical financial reporting control was in 2002.

"Cyber expertise" would follow the similar interpretation given to financial expertise that values true functional depth and understanding of these issues. The proposed rule includes the following non-exclusive list of criteria that a registrant should consider in reaching a determination on whether a director has expertise in cybersecurity:

- Whether the director has prior work experience in cybersecurity, including, for example, prior experience as an information security officer, security policy analyst, security auditor, security architect or engineer, security operations or incident response manager, or business continuity planner;

- Whether the director has obtained a certification or degree in cybersecurity; and

- Whether the director has knowledge, skills, or other background in cybersecurity, including, for example, in the areas of security policy and governance, risk management, security assessment, control evaluation, security architecture and engineering, security operations, incident handling, or business continuity planning.

The similar provision related to financial expertise that was enacted as part of corporate director competency reforms with SOX in 2002 had the effect of "forcing" boards to add significant financial and accounting depth to the boardroom. This was nothing short of transformative for how companies approached financial and accounting controls, systems, policies, procedures and processes not just at the governance level, but it had far reaching management implications over these issues also. Having true cyber expertise on corporate boards would add significant boardroom and management accountability that would likely drive similar levels of functional transformation on cyber security controls, systems, policies, procedures, and processes.

The emerging body of digital and cybersecurity governance standards and leading practices that currently exist are being adopted and implemented voluntarily by some boards. As these practices develop, and even with rating agencies such as ISS that are starting to track and identify cybersecurity-related governance practices, corporate governance reform and corporate director capabilities lag the reality of the digital opportunities and cyber risks facing most organizations.

The most frequently identified digital and cybersecurity governance reforms that are emerging are appearing regularly with regard to board composition, board structure, and risk oversight. Several standard practices have been identified through author assessment of these largely self-regulatory trends. These leading digital and cyber risk governance practices include:

- Boards that ensure corporate directors have the skills and capabilities to understand and govern the complex issues surrounding digital and cybersecurity risk, including adding multiple digitally and cybersecurity savvy directors to the board and disclosing related skills.

- Boards that organize director digital and cybersecurity risk governance activities within a focused technology and cybersecurity committee.

- Directors who understand and govern cyber risk like they do any other financial risk by determining and tracking its potential economic impacts. These directors understand the organization's potential self-insured cyber loss exposure levels and use this information to inform their cyber risk mitigation strategies.

- Directors who identify and govern systemic risk in the organization's complex digital business system as a new dimension in enterprise risk management.

Any corporate board can immediately adopt and build upon these leading practices. Over time, laws and regulations will undoubtedly force board action and reform as the U.S. SEC is now proposing. However, today's market forces and risks warrant an immediate boardroom response to these issues through self-regulated leadership and change.

3.2 Defining the Digitally Savvy Director

Boardroom composition is a foundational issue in corporate governance. The size of the board, who is on it, and the structure of its committees are some of the core issues that shape the capabilities of the boardroom. Board nominating and governance committee's lead on these issues.

In MIT's research on U.S. listed companies and the business impacts of having digitally savvy corporate directors on the board, they define digital competencies "...as an understanding, tested by experience, of how digital technologies such as social, mobile, analytics, cloud, and the Internet of things will impact how companies will succeed in the next decade." They further pinpoint a critical mass of at least three digitally savvy corporate directors as the boardroom tipping point that drives significantly better business outcomes. (Weill *et al.*, 2019, p. 3).

Boardroom effectiveness over any issue starts with the capabilities and diversity of corporate directors. While gender and racial diversity quotas and initiatives are changing board composition, much less is being done on director digital diversity. Competencies to govern the relatively recent and rapid advancement of digital and cybersecurity technologies is not yet a foundational director or boardroom competency present on many corporate boards. Equilar, a corporate leadership data firm, determined for this paper that only 7.7% of the corporate directors in the U.S. Russell 3000 have held job titles, i.e., CIO, CISO, CTO or CDO which would likely categorize them as "digitally savvy" according to the MIT definition (Gomez, 2021).

Compounding the problem is defining what digital competencies are needed in the boardroom. Unlike gender and racial diversity, which are boardroom composition issues that have seen progress over the last decade because of explicit legal reforms, digital diversity is harder to define. Other than the proposed U.S. SEC rules requiring disclosure of cyber expertise, there are no other legal quotas I am aware of that require digital competencies on corporate boards.

Financial expertise was forced into public company boardrooms in the United States with the Sarbanes-Oxley Act of 2002. Financial and accounting expertise and experience is also a well-established professional body of knowledge that is understood and has been taught to other executives in the boardroom as a core part of most business curriculums in higher education. Director digital and cybersecurity competencies still suffer from their absence in formal business educations for most current executives. Casual experiential familiarity and often a negative bias based on a lack of understanding of the typical information technology executives' job such as the CIO or CISO make the issue worse.

Biases from established corporate directors often manifest themselves in the perception that the boardroom does not need "specialist" skills, i.e., CIOs and CISOs, where business strategy, operational, and business value creation competencies are not perceived to be present. This lack of understanding or appreciation for the broad-based business, management, and leadership competencies that are in reality an intrinsic part of these roles is frequently misplaced. Less than two decades ago, it was a novel concept for financial literacy and financial expertise to be in many corporate boardrooms, and it took U.S. legal reforms through SOX to change this. The competencies that these technology executives bring to the boardroom are now as equally fundamental and needed as financial literacy and financial expertise were. See Appendix Exhibit 1 for a typical CIO job description.

The job of the CIO requires an understanding of long-term business goals, the need to team with other executives, effective communications, strong managerial skills, an understanding of regulatory issues, and an ability to govern project outcomes. These competencies and the CIO's depth and familiarity with information technologies and how they create business value translate effectively into the corporate boardroom and responsibilities of corporate directorship.

But more clarity and transparency is needed in what it means to be a digitally savvy director. A boardroom competency model for digital directors needs to reflect the breadth and depth of skills and competencies required to build and sustain any digital business system itself. Leading practices of director skill disclosure and the author's experience with complex digital business systems led to the creation of a competency framework for understanding these issues.

The DiRECTOR framework for governing complex digital business systems discussed in Section 4.8 and seen in Appendix Exhibit 2 also reflects the breadth of director competencies required to govern complex digital business systems. The DiRECTOR framework can be applied as a competency model to understand the digital capabilities needed to govern these issues. This framework was built by understanding the capabilities and approach that the leading corporate boardrooms are already reflecting and pursuing. Digital director's competencies need to span data, information architecture, risk communications, emerging technology, cybersecurity, third-party risk, systemic risk, IT operations, and the regulatory issues related to the digital business system. The notable finding from MIT's research on the correlation between having a critical mass of three digitally savvy directors and the positive business impacts they identified supports an assumption that it would take at least three digitally savvy directors to reflect this breadth of competencies (Zukis, 2021b).

3.3 The Technology and Cybersecurity Committee

Introducing a new committee to improve digital and cybersecurity governance is emerging as a leading practice in the corporate boardroom. U.S. companies such as FedEx, Walmart, GM, AIG, Hasbro, HealthEquity, Transunion, and others have taken this step. Guaranty Trust Bank in Nigeria has also done this. However, it remains a minority practice worldwide and only around 5 percent of the companies in the U.S. R3000 have adopted this practice (MyLogIQ, 2021).

Committees deliver several benefits in corporate governance, including greater knowledge specialization within the committee, task efficiency through the allocation of work related to the monitoring and advising functions of corporate governance, and greater accountability of the board committee to the firm and full board (Chen and Wu, 2016). Other author observed benefits include increased management accountability to the board committee and external signaling to investors and other stakeholders, including potential cyber attackers.

The tradeoff with the segregation of work in a committee is the cost of information asymmetry between committees. This is typically overcome through the mechanism of putting multi-committee directors in place, a practice frequently observed where a technology and cybersecurity committee is present. Commonly, a director working on a technology and cybersecurity committee will share committee assignments with the audit committee, where enterprise risk management oversight responsibilities frequently reside.

It took the Sarbanes-Oxley Act of 2002 to require the creation of an independent audit committee and also mandate that all committee members be financially literate and that at least one be a financial expert. Other committee reforms from SOX introduced a compensation committee and nominating and governance committee. Revisions to the NYSE, NASDAQ listing requirements, and SEC rules followed SOX. These legal reforms introduced a generally accepted committee structure commonly adopted in national codes and adopted by boardrooms around the world. Other committees can also exist on many boards, including risk committees, which are frequently seen on the boards of financial services companies. This practice was driven by regulatory reforms put in place after the financial crisis of 2008.

Charters that define the responsibilities of technology and cybersecurity committees can vary given it is an emerging practice. A model charter has been prepared by reviewing some of the leading practices within U.S. companies that have adopted this committee structure. See Appendix Exhibit 3.

A common existing cyber governance practice is for the audit committee to have responsibility for cyber risk. This is not a recommended practice by U.S. corporate governance leaders Digital Directors Network and the National Association of Corporate Directors for the reasons that it subordinates the cyber risk agenda to the primary financial reporting responsibility of audit committees, and it introduces an inherent competency misalignment between the skills needed to effectively govern cyber risk and the audit and financial expertise that exists on audit committees.

The U.S. SEC's Acting Chief Accountant has also called this practice into question (Munter, 2021):

Without a doubt, today's audit committees have a lot on their plates. Increasingly, audit committees are being tasked with overseeing a company's cybersecurity policies; environment, social, and governance practices; legal and regulatory compliance; and tax risks. While these are most assuredly important issues, and audit committees may be adept at monitoring these risks, we believe it is important that audit committees assess whether the scope of their responsibilities is appropriate, achievable, and aligned with the experience of its members, and importantly, not lose sight of their core responsibility—oversight of financial reporting, including ICFR, engagement of the independent auditor, and oversight of the external audit process.

Organizational design in the boardroom is a critical tool that directly impacts what corporate directors focus on and how they perform their duties. The leading, albeit emergent, practice of putting a technology and cybersecurity committee on the board reflects the real need for more focused attention to the broad and dynamic agenda that encompasses digital and cybersecurity risk oversight.

3.4 Calculating the Projected Economic Losses From Cyber Risk

The cyber insurance industry and some forward-thinking cyber competent boards and management leaders are starting to understand and project cyber risk in economic terms to govern and manage it like any other financial risk.

With the growing acknowledgment that it is not "if" but "when" a company will experience a data breach or cyber-attack, the issue of whether financial statements should reflect contingent liabilities for cyber losses is also a consideration. At present, international accounting standards and practices do not reflect it in my experience. Under U.S. Generally Accepted Accounting Principles (GAAP), companies are currently required to accrue projected losses if a loss is probable (with a greater than 50% likelihood) and the amount of the loss is estimable. Recognizing contingent losses from uncollectable accounts receivables is a typical application of this rule. Loan loss reserves, warranties, product liability, litigation, and losses from property damage are others (FASB of the Financial Accounting Foundation, 2010).

The cyber insurance industry is on the front lines of understanding the economic implications of the cyber risks they have underwritten. However, they are struggling with higher-than-expected cyber losses and are raising rates and reducing coverages (Reuters, 2021a). A key regulator of the insurance industry, the New York Department of Financial Services (NY DFS), released their *Cyber Insurance Risk Framework* to address the insurance industry's shortcomings in understanding the cyber risks they are insuring. Their concerns can be seen in the statement, "Many insurers still have work to do to develop a rigorous and data-driven approach to cyber risk, and experts have expressed concerns that insurers are not yet able to accurately measure cyber risk" (New York State Department of Financial Services, 2021).

The rapidly changing nature of cyber risk makes it challenging, but far from impossible, to determine its potential economic impacts. Moreover, only by understanding cyber risk in the same way as other economic risks can well-informed risk mitigation tactics be implemented that address litigation risk, business risk, and equity risk. Cyber economics is emerging as an extension of applied economics to do this. Cyber economics applies traditional economic theory with statistical methods and data elements specific to cyber risks, such as the growing body of historical threat data, cybersecurity intelligence data, and business-specific data with informed logic models and predictions around economic impacts. Potential cyber-related economic losses can and should be determined and monitored over time reflecting both an organization's cyber control environment and their changing threat landscape.

Estimating cyber losses needs to address the primary financial loss drivers of cyber risk that include ransomware, data breaches, business interruptions, and the misappropriation of assets and intellectual property. Detailed cyber economic loss calculations reflect the probability of the inherent cyber risks that face a company adjusted for the strength of its cyber risk controls, including their corporate governance approach to cybersecurity. The inherent cyber risks reflect the economic business impacts of the unique threat context that faces an organization, including specific industry issues adjusted for the strength of its cyber defense measures and controls. This expected cyber loss or *residual cyber risk* can be monitored and tracked over time, similarly to other potential economic losses. Making this determination can be written as

$$E(Cyber\ Loss) = \Sigma_{i=1}^{7} Residual\ Cyber\ Risk_i * (P)Residual\ Cyber\ Risk_i$$

Cyber Economic Loss Formula Provided by Digital Directors Network and X-Analytics

Once determined and expressed in financial terms, expected cyber loss impacts can be segmented by economic loss type to inform and guide risk management activities such as transfer, mitigation, or acceptance. Once expected cyber losses are contextualized in economic terms, risk management activities can be applied in the context of where financial exposure lies to accommodate corporate board determined thresholds for risk appetite and risk tolerance.

Critical to these estimates is the realization that the organization's vast majority of economic loss from cyber risk is self-insured. Based on author estimates, less than 10 percent of the potential economic losses related to cyber risk have been insured in the United States. Corporate boards will not understand the implications of cyber risk until they begin to understand the potential economic value that is at risk beyond the risk that has been transferred through cyber insurance.

3.5 Governing Systemic Risk in Complex Digital Business Systems

In December of 2020, Collins J. Seitz, the U.S. Delaware Supreme Court Chief Justice, said in an interview that "Boards must be able to demonstrate credibly that they're thinking proactively about potential systemic risks" (Lewis, 2020).

The world is full of complex systems, natural ones such as the planetary system and humanmade ones such as the digital business systems that enable and power most companies. The intrinsic systemic risks within complex systems relate to the observation that complex systems have inherent levels of risk embedded in the very nature of the complex system. These risks are systemic because failure of one part of a system can trigger "domino effects" or the potential for cascading impacts and more extensive failures throughout the much larger system. The non-linear nature of systemic risk is one of its hallmarks, as is the difficultly of understanding and predicting systemic risk levels and their extended impacts. In complex systems, small events or failures can significantly and negatively impact the more extensive system (Zukis et al., 2022).

In 1986 the U.S. Space Shuttle Challenger exploded shortly after lift-off, killing the seven astronauts on board. The infamous "O-ring" failure in the Challenger's thrust system caused the entire complex system of the shuttle to fail catastrophically. While not related to the Shuttle's digital system, this simple mechanical failure illustrates the principles behind systemic risk. Systemic risk reflects the inherent risks that exist in and between the parts of a complex system that threatens the purpose of the system.

In 2009, as the worst of the global economic crisis known as "The Great Recession" started to recede and research into the crisis led central bankers from around the world to develop the standard known as Basel III. Basel III was intended to mitigate systemic risk in the global banking sector. Focused on strengthening the resilience of individual banks, Basel III addressed the concept of "too big to fail" by studying what contributed to the crisis and building capability that could identify and reduce systemic risk within the banking sector to prevent future economic disasters in the global financial system. Public financial services companies in the U.S. now address and disclose their systemically important role in the capital markets system in regulatory filings.

The global banking industry also now has a much better understanding of systemic risk throughout the global financial system. Global systemically important banks and financial institutions are now identified and monitored by the Financial Stability Board (FSB). The FSB is an international body that works with national financial authorities and standard setters to monitor and make recommendations about the global financial system. Its decisions are not legally binding on its members; they are instead bound by a shared dependency of a well-functioning global financial system (Financial Stability Board, 2020).

There is not yet a similar body focused on the systemic risks inherent throughout the connected digital world. Industry groups and business ecosystems may begin to form similar bodies to help govern and understand systemic risks throughout their extended ecosystems.

COVID-19 is a catastrophic systemic failure of healthcare systems around the world. Systemic risk within healthcare systems and the critical constraint of providing intensive care at scale created cascading problems for the entire healthcare system. As the toll of COVID-19 started to explode at the beginning of the pandemic, the threat of healthcare systems starting to fail become real. Reactions and decisions taken to this risk in healthcare triggered actions that then started a cascade of systemic impacts as risk spread and entered many other complex systems causing damage and disruption to worldwide economic, social, political, and business systems.

Late in 2020, it was discovered that the SolarWinds Orion software product, which manages and optimizes IT environments for thousands of customers and government agencies, had been corrupted and made into a weapon that attackers leveraged to attack SolarWinds client base. The corruption of this critical part of SolarWinds digital business system gave attackers an efficient and systemic way to "piggyback" through a key process that would gain them trusted access into the SolarWinds customer base. This efficiently scaled their attack to create as much damage as possible (Panettieri, 2021).

The hack into Colonial Pipeline's network in 2021, reportedly through the simple vulnerability of a compromised password, caused the largest fuel pipeline in the United States to be shut down barely an hour after the ransomware attack was initiated. Colonial's leadership decided to shut down their pipeline, and later that day, its CEO decided to pay the USD 4.4 million ransomware demand (Turton and Mehrotra, 2021). However, not before the shutdown created systemic damage with fuel shortages and widespread disruption well beyond the controlled shutdown of the pipeline. The CEO decided to pay the ransomware extortion and bring the pipeline back online after admitting the company did not understand the risks related to the hack (Eaton and Volz, 2021). A simple password failure, together with a lack of understanding of the risks that their complex digital business system could carry into their operating pipelines, created an operating system shutdown that had far-reaching systemic effects that negatively impacted millions of people and businesses.

In situations where systemic risk is not understood in complex systems, leadership generally has two decision paths when the system begins to fail. First, ignore the risk and let the failures and their implications run their course. Second, shut the system down. Political leaders in the United States and worldwide chose both of those two paths as COVID-19 was spiraling out of control in 2020. The U.S. federal government initially chose to ignore the risk, while some states took the other path and shut down most social interactions with stay-at-home orders.

CNA Insurance, a top 10 cyber insurer in the U.S., suffered a ransomware attack in 2021 and reportedly ended up paying USD 40 million in ransom to bring their systems back online (Mehrotra and Turton, 2021). Reports indicated that attackers could have been interested in identifying customers who were insured against cyber risk to identify their terms of coverage (Hope, 2021). This would have allowed attackers to target these customers with a ransomware attack specific to the insurance policy coverages that CNA Insurance had underwritten. However, CNA has disclosed that they do not believe policyholder data was targeted or misused (CNA Financial Corporation, 2021). Attackers who exploit a weakness or leverage point in one part of a complex digital business system to inflict much broader damage across the system reflects the definition of systemic risk.

As defined in the context of digital business systems, a *system* is a "Combination of interacting elements organized to achieve one or more stated purposes" (ISO/IEC/IEEE 15288, 2015, First Edition, p. 9). The interacting elements that compose a digital system include hardware, software, data, humans, processes, procedures, facilities, materials, and naturally occurring entities.

Built-up and evolving over time, digital business systems contain massive amounts of data and collections of disparate and interconnected parts. They are complex because of the rules and regulations that dictate their design and purpose and their dependencies on third parties who are part of the inter-connected system. Moreover, the diverse

3.5. Governing Systemic Risk in Complex Digital Business Systems

skills, practices, and policies needed to manage and secure the system compounds its complexity and increases inherent levels of systemic risk within the system.

The inherent complexity of the modern digital business system is introducing a level of vulnerability and risk that has not previously existed for companies, economies, and societies. Systemic risk exists in many other complex systems built by humankind from healthcare to transportation, to energy. The increasing dependency of each of these systems on complex information systems has intertwined many different types of risks to create an unprecedented level of systemic risk worldwide.

Systemic risk is a new dimension of enterprise risk that most boards and organizations do not yet understand, govern, or manage. Lack of disclosure is one indication of this, as is the emphasis regulators are putting on the cyber insurance industry to understand it. The NY DFS *Cyber Insurance Risk Framework* explicitly addresses systemic risk and the growing risk that these threats introduce to the cyber insurance risk transfer industry (New York State Department of Financial Services, 2021):

> As part of their cyber insurance risk strategy, insurers that offer cyber insurance should regularly evaluate systemic risk and plan for potential losses. Systemic risk has grown in part because institutions increasingly rely on third-party vendors and those vendors are highly concentrated in key areas like cloud services and managed services providers. Insurers should understand the critical third parties used by their insureds and model the effect of a catastrophic cyber event on such critical third parties that may cause simultaneous losses to many of their insureds. Examples of such events could include a self-propagating malware, such as NotPetya, or a supply chain attack, such as the SolarWinds trojan, that infects many institutions at the same time, or a cyber event that disables a major cloud services provider. A catastrophic cyber event could inflict

tremendous losses on insurers that may jeopardize their financial solvency.

Third-party risk is only one aspect of systemic risk within complex digital business systems. There is also systemic risk inherent throughout the system. Systemic risk can relate to data corruption or failure of a software component in one part of the system that creates risks that spread and degrade the performance of the more extensive system. Systemic risk increases with the integration of information technology and operational technology, introducing widespread risks that can impair foundational business processes and critical infrastructure (Zukis, 2020).

Corporate disclosure of systemic risk also indicates how immature governance and management activities are currently around this issue. While financial services firms address systemic risk in the context of their role in the capital markets due to the regulatory reforms put in place after 2008, systemic risk disclosures in the context of the digital business system are virtually non-existent in the United States. Based upon a review of the risk disclosures of companies in the U.S. R3000 index, Walmart was identified as the only company that makes a comprehensive systemic risk disclosure within the context of their digital business system (author emphasis) (Walmart Inc., 2021, p. 19):

> Our compliance programs, information technology, and enterprise risk management efforts **cannot eliminate all systemic risk.** Disruptions in our systems caused by security breaches or cyberattacks – **including attacks on those parties we do business with** – could harm our ability to conduct our operations, which may have a material effect on us, may result in losses that could have a material adverse effect on our financial position or results of operations, or may have a **cascading effect that adversely impacts our partners, third-party service providers, customers, financial services firms, and other third parties that we interact with on a regular basis.**
>
> In addition, such security-related events could be widely publicized and could materially adversely affect our reputation with our customers, members, associates, vendors

3.5. Governing Systemic Risk in Complex Digital Business Systems 45

and shareholders, **could harm our competitive position particularly with respect to our eCommerce operations, and could result in a material reduction in our net sales in our eCommerce operations, as well as in our stores thereby materially adversely affecting our operations, net sales, results of operations, financial position, cash flows and liquidity.** Such events could also result in the release to the public of confidential information about our operations and financial position and performance and could result in **litigation** or other legal actions against us or the imposition of penalties, fines, fees or liabilities, **which may not be covered by our insurance policies.** Moreover, a security compromise or ransomware event could require us to **devote significant management resources** to address the problems created by the issue and to **expend significant additional resources** to upgrade further the security measures we employ to guard personal and confidential information against cyberattacks and other attempts to access or otherwise compromise such information and could result in a disruption of our operations, particularly our digital operations.

This disclosure reflects the foundational inability of Walmart to completely eliminate systemic risk and its material and far-reaching impacts. Along with addressing multiple business risks, the disclosure also addresses litigation risk and Walmart's self-insured exposure to these risks.

Investor disclosures are a potential useful indicator of how well boards and companies understand systemic risk and its implications for business, litigation, and equity risk. Accurate and meaningful disclosure is an expectation and requirement to protect investor interests in public companies and is a foundation of public capital markets worldwide.

The work done after "The Great Recession" to understand systemic risk in capital markets and the complex inter-connected financial industry demonstrates that it is possible to understand and mitigate systemic risk. This work now needs to expand into other domains beyond the financial system. All of our humanmade systems constantly evolve to serve a changing and growing collection of needs and wants and the systemic risks inherent within them will also continue to evolve and grow alongside this evolution.

Incident disclosure practices also remain inconsistent as several SEC enforcement actions and fines in the United States have identified weaknesses in cyber incident disclosure controls (Patterson Balknap Webb and Tyler, LLP., 2021). Rapid disclosure of incidents is also a tactic in mitigating systemic cyber risk. The SEC wants companies to provide cybersecurity disclosures that are specific to the organization. They do not want generic disclosure, but they acknowledge the need to walk the fine line of providing a "roadmap" that could make the company more susceptible to a cybersecurity incident. The 2018 SEC guidance also explicitly requests U.S. public companies to consider the range of harm that could be caused to customers and suppliers in determining materiality, i.e., systemic impact. In August 2021, Pearson plc (NYSE: PSO), a UK company that trades on the London Stock Exchange and also lists its American Depository Receipts on the New York Stock Exchange, settled charges for US$ 1 million that it misled investors related to a 2018 cyber intrusion involving the theft of millions of student data records (U.S. Securities and Exchange Commission, 2022a).

Some companies are doing a much better job on cyber risk disclosure than others. FedEx (NYSE: FDX), a company that receives an "A" grading on their boardroom digital and cybersecurity policies and practices (Digital Directors Network, 2021b), made the following cybersecurity-related Form 10-K disclosure for their fiscal year ended May 31, 2021 (FedEx Corporation, 2022):

> **A significant data breach or other disruption to our technology infrastructure could disrupt our operations and result in the loss of critical confidential information, adversely impacting our reputation, business or results of operations.**
>
> Our ability to attract and retain customers, to efficiently operate our businesses, and to compete effectively depends in

part upon the sophistication, security and reliability of our technology network, including our ability to provide features of service that are important to our customers, to protect our confidential business information and the information provided by our customers, and to maintain customer confidence in our ability to protect our systems and to provide services consistent with their expectations. For example, we rely on information technology to receive package level information in advance of physical receipt of packages, to track items that move through our delivery systems, to efficiently plan deliveries, to execute billing processes, and to track and report financial and operational data. We are subject to risks imposed by data breaches and operational disruptions, including through cyberattack or cyber-intrusion, including by computer hackers, foreign governments, cyber terrorists, cyber criminals and malicious employees or other insiders of FedEx or third-party service providers. Data breaches of companies and governments have increased in recent years as the number, intensity and sophistication of attempted attacks and intrusions from around the world have increased and we, our customers and third parties increasingly store and transmit data by means of connected information technology systems. Additionally, risks such as code anomalies, "Acts of God," transitional challenges in migrating operating company functionality to our FedEx enterprise automation platforms, data leakage, cyber-fraud and human error pose a direct threat to our products, services, systems and data and could result in unauthorized or block legitimate access to sensitive or confidential data regarding our operations, customers, employees and suppliers, including personal information.

The technology infrastructure of acquired businesses, as well as their practices related to the use and maintenance of data, could also present issues that we were not able to identify prior to the acquisition. See "Failure to successfully implement our business strategy and effectively respond to changes in market dynamics and customer preferences will cause our future financial results to suffer." below for additional information on risks related to our recent acquisition of ShopRunner and launch of FedEx Dataworks.

We also depend on and interact with the technology and systems of third parties, including our customers and third-party service providers such as cloud service providers and delivery services. Such third parties may host, process or have access to information we maintain about our company, customers, employees and vendors or operate systems that are critical to our business operations and services. Like us, these third parties are subject to risks imposed by data breaches, cyberattacks and other events or actions that could damage, disrupt or close down their networks or systems. We have security processes, protocols and standards in place, including contractual provisions requiring such security measures, that are applicable to such third parties and are designed to protect information that is held by them, or to which they have access, as a result of their engagements with us. Nevertheless, a cyberattack could defeat one or more of such third parties' security measures, allowing an attacker to obtain information about our company, customers, employees and vendors or disrupt our operations. These third parties may also experience operational disruptions or human error that could result in unauthorized access to sensitive or confidential data regarding our operations, customers, employees and suppliers, including personal information.

A disruption to our complex, global technology infrastructure, including those impacting our computer systems and websites, could result in the loss of confidential business or customer information, require substantial repairs or replacements, resulting in significant costs, and lead to the temporary or permanent transfer by customers of some or

3.5. Governing Systemic Risk in Complex Digital Business Systems 49

all of their business to our competitors. The foregoing could harm our reputation and adversely impact our operations, customer service and results of operations. Additionally, a security breach could require us to devote significant management resources to address the problems created. These types of adverse impacts could also occur in the event the confidentiality, integrity or availability of company and customer information was compromised due to a data loss by FedEx or a trusted third party. We or the third parties with which we share information may not discover any security breach and loss of information for a significant period of time after the security breach occurs.

We have invested and continue to invest in technology security initiatives, information-technology risk management, business continuity and disaster recovery plans, including investments to retire and replace end-of-life systems. The development and maintenance of these measures is costly and requires ongoing monitoring and updating as technologies change and efforts to overcome security measures become increasingly more frequent, intense and sophisticated. Despite our efforts, we are not fully insulated from data breaches, technology disruptions, data loss and cyber-fraud, which could adversely impact our competitiveness and results of operations. For instance, in 2017 TNT Express worldwide operations were significantly affected due to the infiltration of an information-technology virus known as NotPetya. In 2017 FedEx was one of many companies attacked by the rapidly spreading ransomware described as WannaCry that exploited vulnerability in a third-party software program and infected computers using that program, encrypting files and holding them for ransom. During 2018, we discovered an unsecured server hosted by one of our third-party cloud service providers, which exposed some archived account information related to a service discontinued after our 2015 acquisition of Bongo International, LLC. The server has been secured, and we have found no indication that any information has been misappropriated in connection with the incident. Additionally, we have experienced continual attempts by cyber criminals, some of which were successful, to gain access to customer accounts for the purposes of fraudulently diverting and misappropriating items being transported in our network. None of the WannaCry ransomware attack, unsecured server or fraudulent cyber activities caused a material disruption to our systems or resulted in any material costs to FedEx.

While we have significant security processes and initiatives in place, we may be unable to detect or prevent a breach or disruption in the future. Additionally, while we have insurance coverage designed to address certain aspects of cyber risks in place, such insurance coverage may be insufficient to cover all losses or all types of claims that may arise. See "Our business is subject to complex and evolving U.S. and foreign laws and regulations regarding data protection." below for additional information on risks related to legal and regulatory developments with respect to data protection.

This comprehensive cyber risk disclosure reflects digital issues specific to FedEx, along with the vital role their digital business system has throughout their business. The FedEx disclosure explicitly addresses issues in systemic risk along with the inherited cyber risks related to acquisitions. This is a lesson they learned when they suffered a ransomware attack during 2017 in their TNT Dutch subsidiary, an acquisition they made the year before. As a result of the attack, they disclosed USD 300 million in operational impacts along with the fact that they did not have cyber insurance at the time. They now disclose that they have cyber insurance in this recent disclosure.

In addition to this comprehensive disclosure, the FedEx board organizes digital and cybersecurity risk oversight through a Cyber and Technology Oversight Committee with a comprehensive charter applied by four self-reported digitally savvy directors who they believe bring deep and broad digital expertise and experience to the FedEx boardroom. The former chair of this committee at FedEx, John Inglis, was appointed as the first U.S. National Cyber Director by President Joe Biden and advises the President on cybersecurity policy and strategy (The White House, 2022).

FedEx's leading self-regulatory approach to digital and cyber risk is an exception. Similar policies and practices are observed elsewhere and are addressed in the next section. Collectively, these leading practices offer a blueprint that regulators and any corporate board can follow to rapidly advance digital and cyber risk oversight.

4

Self-Regulation: National Codes and Other Standards

The explicit reference to digital or cyber risk or specific governance expectations in national codes worldwide is the rare exception, not the rule. Where digital and cybersecurity governance practices are in place in the boardroom, they are being implemented voluntarily by progressive boards innovating into the issues as they learn from and create leading practices along the way. This self-regulated approach has not created broad based boardroom transformation in digital and cyber risk oversight. Legal requirements such as corporate laws, listing requirements, or other "hard law" directives that impose specific digital and cybersecurity governance requirements on boardrooms and corporate directors are not yet common.

However, some of the self-regulating digital and cyber governance standards and codes that do exist are fairly comprehensive and some have existed for a relatively long time. Along with these voluntary standards, a collection of common leading practices is starting to emerge. Together, these precedents offer a roadmap for the development of digital and cybersecurity governance policies and practices.

This section explores these voluntary standards and highlights the developing nature of regulatory views in several economies worldwide. Not intended to be a comprehensive review of all legal and regulatory jurisdictions, this analysis identifies key pieces to the puzzle to create a mosaic of how digital and cybersecurity governance is evolving, and can further develop worldwide.

While broad based global regulatory reform in digital and cybersecurity governance is not yet happening, there is a rapidly expanding amount of legislation already imposing data privacy and cybersecurity rules onto management teams and their organizations. These laws are being implemented to hold corporations to new levels of digital and data accountability and codify citizens' rights around their data. The Global Data Protection Regulation (GDPR) was adopted in 2016 by the European Union and has served as a model for many other data protection regulations worldwide, such as the California Consumer Privacy Act (CCPA). CCPA went into effect in 2020. Over €1.6 billion of fines have been levied under GDPR through April 2022 (CMS Law, 2022).

China's Personal Information Protection Law (PIPL) went into effect on November 1, 2021. It imposed far-reaching requirements and significant penalties of up to 5% of annual revenue on information processors within and without China (Dezan Shira & Associates, 2021). The law also provides for individual liability and requires information processors to conduct compliance audits and impact assessments. China's Data Security Law (DSL) went into effect in September of 2021 and introduced new rules for any company operating in China on how they process and protect data. The DSL also introduced new civil and criminal penalties for noncompliance (Jones Day, 2021).

While most of these laws do not directly enact or create corporate governance reforms, they all impact the responsibilities of the board and corporate directors to understand and govern how their companies comply with the laws and address these issues. Global regulators have recognized that digital and cybersecurity issues have implications that are in the interests of the public, investors, the economy, and national security.

With the slow pace of digital and cyber governance reform the boardroom is lagging the national strategies that are being established around the world to create long-term sustainable digital economies. These initiatives require private-sector leadership, involvement, and support in order for digital economies to emerge and thrive sustainably. This is causing the gap to expand between the boardroom's ability to govern digital and cyber risk and the real market, litigation and business risks facing organizations and management teams as a result of their digital business systems.

Leaving digital and cybersecurity governance reform up to voluntary self-regulated transformation will mean that the pace of change remains slow, guaranteeing that the gap between effective governance and risk will continue to grow. Given what is at stake, the author believes there needs to be more corporate governance focused legal and regulatory reform to rapidly advance boardroom transformation and close this gap. Policy recommendations in Section 5 reflect a range of suggested "hard" and "soft" corporate governance reforms for regulators and corporate boards worldwide.

National codes and standards in digital and cybersecurity governance can vary widely, and the development of the guidance so far is fairly arbitrary. The adoption of leading digital governance policies and practices in the boardroom is equally irregular. However, the national codes that do explicitly address digital and cybersecurity governance can provide insight to any corporate director to consider in the context of their own boardroom. By viewing these practices and policies as leading practices to be learned from, corporate directors have the ability to self-regulate and materially improve their approach to governing these issues.

The following analysis is not intended to be an inventory of every explicit digital or cyber requirement or reference in the many national corporate governance codes or laws that exist around the world. These observations highlight and illustrate the main trends in director skills, boardroom structure, and scope of risk disclosure from a collection of nations who are on a faster track towards corporate governance reform in these areas.

4.1 Australia

Recognized as the world's first ICT-focused corporate governance standard, *AS8015 Corporate Governance of Information and Communication*

Technology formalized the first structured governance approach to help corporate directors govern information technology when it was published in 2005.

AS8015 was intended to be a universal standard for public and private companies, government entities, and not-for-profits regardless of size. Widely acclaimed, *AS8015* would go on to be the blueprint that was adopted by the International Organization for Standardization (ISO) as *ISO/IEC 38500* in May 2008. A second edition was published in 2015. *AS8015* now aligns with the ISO standard. This leading practice standard, *ISO/IEC 38500:2015* represents one of the most mature and comprehensive ICT governance standards worldwide. The standard is currently being reviewed as part of ISO's regular five-year review cycle. Details of some of its features are addressed in Section 4.7.

4.2 Japan

Changes to Japan's Corporate Governance Code have been made as a result of the Tokyo Stock Exchange's (TSE) market segmentation initiative which was implemented on April 4, 2022. Reorganizing into three market segments; Prime Market, Standard Market, and Growth Market, companies wishing to be listed in the TSE's Prime Market segment have now had to strengthen their corporate governance policies and practices. The goal behind the stock exchange reorganization and the commensurate raising of corporate governance standards is for Japanese companies to better meet the needs of global institutional investors (Institutional Investor, 2021).

Guidelines for "Investor and Company Engagement" under Japan's Corporate Governance Code now include explicit expectations on digital and cybersecurity. The following revision has been included within the supplemental investor engagement guidelines under the category of "Management Decisions in Response to Changes in the Business Environment" (author emphasis) (Revisions of Japan's Corporate Governance Code and Guidelines for Investor and Company Engagement, (2021)):

Does the company appropriately respond to changes in the environment surrounding the business, such as increasing social demand for and interest in [Environmental, Social and Governance] ESG and [Sustainable Development Goals] SDGs, **progress in digital transformation, the need to address cyber security**, and the need for fair and appropriate transactions throughout the supply chain in its management strategies and plans? Further, does the company have a structure in place, such as the establishment of a committee on sustainability under the board or the management side, to review and promote sustainability-related initiatives on an enterprise-wide basis? [Provisional Translation]

The Japanese Code follows the "comply or explain" principle to drive thoughtful governance around oversight. While not prescriptive in requiring structured corporate governance reform in digital and cyber risk oversight, the Japanese Code nonetheless is directed towards greater investor engagement and disclosure in the company's path towards safely shaping their digital future. Engaging investors on both digital transformation and cyber risk is a strong leading worldwide practice in corporate governance.

4.3 Malaysia

The *Malaysian Code On Corporate Governance (MCCG)* was updated in April 2021 and included several explicit references to cyber risk governance including recommending a risk management committee that includes cyber security within its scope (author emphasis) (Securities Commission Malaysia, 2021):

The board should, in its disclosure, include a discussion on how key risk areas such as finance, operations, regulatory compliance, reputation, **cyber security** and sustainability were evaluated and the controls in place to mitigate or manage those risks. In addition, it should state if the risk management framework adopted by the company is based on an internationally recognised risk management framework.

The MCCG also recommends that "good cyber hygiene practices are in place including data privacy and security to prevent cyber threats" along with the suggestion for listed companies to leverage technology to facilitate voting and remote shareholder participation. The MCCG notably moves cyber security out from underneath the audit committee with the risk committee alignment and guidance on how cyber risk management should be governed and managed.

Notably, the Malaysian code is not based on the "comply or explain" principle common in many other countries. It adopts the CARE principle, or Comprehend, Apply and Report, an "apply or explain an alternative" principle. Instead of explaining the reasons for non-compliance, CARE is intended to identify the thought processes and provide a meaningful explanation for the corporate governance practices utilized.

In addition to the MCCG recommending that boards of listed companies adopt a risk management committee it encourages private companies to follow the code. Governing information security risk in a risk management committee, and assuming the committee members have the requisite cyber competencies to understand these issues, would allow for more focus and better alignment than the common worldwide practice of tasking cyber risk to an audit committee.

Malaysia's largest bank and one of its most prominent companies, Maybank (Malayan Banking Berhad), does just that. In their disclosures under the MCCG that describe their Risk Management Committee's (RMC) responsibility, they disclose, "The RMC is responsible for formulating policies and frameworks to identify, measure, monitor, manage and control the material risk components impacting the businesses including IT-related risk" (Malayan Banking Berhad, 2020, p. 52). The Maybank board has 12 directors and six RMC members. The RMC held ten meetings during the year with 100% attendance.

Specific training and education course/event disclosures are also made for each director during the year. Four directors attended cyber-specific training events, including the chairman. Course or event disclosures include: "Cybercrime," "Cybersecurity & Work-From-Home

Security Challenges Amidst COVID-19 Pandemic," "Cybersecurity Challenges & Response," and "Cyber Security in the Boardroom."

Disclosing corporate directors' specific actions to remain current and informed is not a commonly observed disclosure practice. However, the disclosure of director training, including cybersecurity courses alongside the stated governance responsibility within the committee charter for "IT-related risk," are leading practices in a digital and cybersecurity governance system to demonstrate the efforts corporate directors are making to understand and effectively govern issues relevant to the company.

4.4 Nigeria

The *Nigerian Code of Corporate Governance 2018 (NCCG)* adopts an "apply and explain" principle to its standards. In the overall charter for the board, the NCCG plainly states that the board's responsibilities include "providing oversight of Information Technology governance" (Financial Reporting Council of Nigeria, 2018, Section 1.10).

The Code makes a strong recommendation that the Board should consider a risk management committee and within this committee, the Code explicitly addresses the oversight of information technology, both its upsides and downsides within the scope of this committee's mandate. Where a risk committee and audit committee both exist, the Code recommends at least one multi-committee director to reduce information asymmetries between these two committees.

The Code also requires the chair of the risk committee to be a non-executive director and a requirement to meet at least twice per year. The Code recommends alignment with business strategy, the performance of IT, third-party risk, and cyber threats as core boardroom oversight areas. The Code also requires periodic independent assessment of the company's IT activities. Recommendations for this committee include (Financial Reporting Council of Nigeria, 2018, Section 11.5.6.6):

> Review and recommend for approval of the Board, at least annually, the Company's Information Technology (IT) data

governance framework to ensure that IT data risks are adequately mitigated and relevant assets are managed effectively. The framework may include:

(1) (a) Development of IT strategy and policy;
(2) (b) Proactive monitoring and management of cyber threats and attacks as well as adverse social media incidents;
(3) (c) Management of risks relating to third-party and outsourced IT service providers;
(4) (d) Assessment of value delivered to the Company through investments in IT; and
(5) (e) Periodic independent assurance on the effectiveness of the Company's IT arrangements.

Guaranty Trust Bank, Nigeria's largest company with almost US$ 2.5 billion in revenue, has a Board Risk Management Committee tasked with a wide range of risks, including credit risk, reputational risk, operations risk, technology risk, market risk and liquidity risk.

However, they also have a Board Information Technology Strategy Committee to bring even more focus to the governance of the specific digital issues and risks impacting the bank. With seven committee members, it met twice during the year ended December 31, 2020. Three of these committee members are multi-committee directors with their Board Risk Management Committee. They also disclose in their annual report that they provide training for all staff that includes cybersecurity and corporate governance.

The scope of responsibility for this dedicated IT committee is disclosed as (Guaranty Trust Bank plc., 2021, p. 18):

> The Board Information Technology Strategy Committee is responsible for the provision of strategic guidance to Management on Information Technology issues and monitoring the effectiveness and efficiency of Information Technology within the Bank and the adequacy of controls.

The Terms of Reference of the Board Information Technology Strategy Committee include:

- Provide advice on the strategic direction of Information Technology issues in the Bank;
- Inform and advise the Board on important Information Technology issues in the Bank;
- Monitor overall Information Technology performance and practices in the Bank.

Guaranty Trust Bank plc also makes a specific systemic risk management disclosure statement in their annual report. While not uncommon to be mentioned in financial services firm disclosure statements in the context of a bank's systemic role within capital markets, Guaranty Trust Bank also references cyber risk within the overall statement on systemic risk management:

> **Systemic risk management:** The Bank's Enterprise Risk Management (ERM) division works with relevant units in the bank in managing risks in our business operations and activities. There are several risk management units in charge of managing different risks such as environmental and social, credit, operational, reputational, market, legal, cyber risks, among others (p. 37).

Guaranty Trust Bank's digital and cybersecurity governance practices go beyond the national code. A dedicated Board Information Technology Strategy Committee reflects a leading worldwide practice in digital and cybersecurity risk oversight.

4.5 South Africa

The *King IV Report on Corporate Governance for South Africa (King IV Report)* replaced King III in its entirety in 2016. King IV, like many national codes, is a voluntary set of principles and leading practices. It offers a progressive and comprehensive standard around ICT governance and is one of the world's most comprehensive standards in this regard.

King IV is a leading national framework in ICT, and its ICT governance elements were first introduced with King III in 2009. As a mature and comprehensive ICT standard, it is well integrated within the broader general corporate governance principles of South Africa. King IV presents a clear case for technology and information governance that is being driven by "advances in data analytics, the Internet of things, robotics, artificial intelligence, 3D printing, nanotechnology, and biotechnology and their profound impacts on supply chains, industries, and business models" (Institute of Directors In Southern Africa NPC, 2016).

Within King, IV is the declaration that "Technology is now part of the corporate DNA. Thus, the security of information systems has become critical. Technology governance and security should become another recurring item on the governing body's agenda" (p. 10). This statement articulates the importance of, and urgent need for corporate governance reform in digital and cybersecurity governance policies and practices around the world.

King IV made a shift from the principle of "apply or explain" to "apply and explain." This shift requires more thoughtful corporate governance from directors and brings greater transparency to the board's thinking in applying the King IV principles and practices. The core King IV technology and information governance principle includes eight recommended practices. These cover boardroom accountability, a wide range of specific oversight responsibilities, outcomes related to information architecture, privacy and security, and emerging technology. The board receiving independent assurance on the organization's technology and information effectiveness and disclosure of overview practices, incidents, performance assessments, and future plans are also recommendations. King IV also covers critical digital governance responsibilities in business resilience, third-party risk, the integrated system of people, process and technology, technology ethics, return on investments, and technology disposal. This suggested depth and breadth of information technology oversight stands out amongst countries worldwide.

As an outcome-focused set of principles, several specific tactics related to digital and cybersecurity governance were rejected during public commentary for King IV. During the public comment period

4.5. South Africa

for King IV, it was suggested that King IV be more prescriptive in requiring information and communication technology competencies in board composition. The King Committee rejected this as too prescriptive and broad to implement because it could potentially introduce an infinite set of specialist skills to be considered. Instead, King IV leaves this issue up to the governing body to determine the requisite ICT skills required on the board.

It was also suggested that King IV should recommend an IT Committee. Again, this was not incorporated into the code to be consistent with the fact that King IV is generally non-prescriptive in any committee recommendations, once again leaving this up to the governing body on a needs basis (Institute of Directors Sourthern Africa KING IV, 2016).

Shoprite, one of South Africa's largest public companies and Africa's largest fast-moving consumer goods retailer, prepares a comprehensive King IV compliance report. They also prepare an annual report filed according to the rules of the Johannesburg Stock Exchange. They have identified information and technology as the fourth most material issue facing the company. They disclose several specific upside and downside issues that are driving the materiality of these risks to their business as well as enhancements to their IT governance (Shoprite Holdings Ltd., 2020, p. 45):

> Continued investment in technology and data analysis remains a priority as the Group strategically positions itself for optimising the business to create new opportunities and grow into new markets. The initial disruptions caused by the implementation of the integrated ERP system in FY 2019 have been addressed. The system has led to significant improvements in operational efficiency, enhanced customer insight and data analytics, and the ability to roll out technology-based initiatives at scale and on demand. This is shown in certain brands being able to target new market segments and the use of real-time inventory data to optimise and manage stock levels. Greater emphasis has

been placed on our IT governance – with a focus on data security and privacy – to provide appropriate and sustainable IT governance.

Their disclosure of the significant business risks that accompany a large-scale digital systems project, such as enterprise resource planning (ERP) system implementation is notable. In describing the information technology and cyber risks that Shoprite is facing, their annual report also makes the following disclosure:

> IT and cyber risk includes any threat to Shoprite's business data, critical systems and business processes associated with the adoption of, operation, ownership and use of information technology. This risk includes compromised business data due to unauthorised access or use, failure to protect data and prevent cyberattacks, an inability to access IT systems needed for business operations, and reduced productivity due to slow or delayed access to IT systems (p. 49).

As a somewhat generic statement, this risk disclosure does not address outbound or inbound systemic risks. According to their King IV report, Shoprite tasks their Audit and Risk Committee (ARC) with IT governance. The ARC charter explicitly addresses their responsibilities related to IT governance. Moreover, the ARC requires that at least one-third of its members have expertise or experience in information technology and information systems, amongst other skills. They have three committee members on their ARC for an eight-person board. However, director skill disclosures in information technology or information systems are not present, including cybersecurity competencies, training, or education.

The ARC committee monitors and evaluates significant IT investments at every meeting, reviews IT risks including disaster recovery, monitors asset management, system availability, global data leakage prevention, and legal and regulatory compliance issues according to their King IV compliance report (Shoprite Holdings Ltd., 2020).

Shoprite's disclosures reflect the positive impact that a comprehensive "self-regulated" national code such as King IV can have to drive precise levels of boardroom accountability and breadth and depth around

4.6. The United States

digital and cybersecurity risk oversight. However, observed gaps in director expertise and experience in information management and information systems fall short of global leading practices, suggesting potential weaknesses in the application of their digital and cybersecurity oversight policies. But generally, both KING IV and Shoprite's digital and cybersecurity governance policies and practices are significantly more mature than most standards or practices for companies around the world.

4.6 The United States

The United States is a corporate governance laggard in many respects in digital and cybersecurity risk oversight. That might be about to change as proposed SEC rules would significantly change how U.S. public company boardrooms govern these issues.

As the most cyber-attacked country in the world, the United States national cyber and corporate weaknesses are no secret to attackers (Ang, 2021). Regulatory mandates in cyber governance or the widespread adoption of voluntary codes or other leading practices within most U.S. boardrooms lags the reality of this risk environment. Recently suggested SEC legal reforms could change this quickly.

A small body of leading digital and cyber governance practices is however emerging from a few well-known U.S. companies. These boardroom policies are mature enough to be assessed and graded to document a standard in digital and cyber risk governance that other boardrooms can learn from (Table 4.1). Several leaders and their reported grades include:

Table 4.1: Digital and cybersecurity governance grades determined by qualitative assessment of boardroom skills, structure and scope of risk disclosure by Digital Directors Network

Company	Card Grade
Citrix, Inc. (NASDAQ: CTXS)	A
FedEx, Inc. (NYSE: FDX)	A
GM, Inc. (NYSE: GM)	B+
HealthEquity, Inc. (NASDAQ: HQY)	B+
Hasbro, Inc. (NASDAQ: HAS)	B

Source: Digital Directors Network (2021b).

The boardroom policies and practices of these companies reflect a system of digital and cybersecurity risk oversight that starts with corporate directors who have both breadth and depth in digital expertise. These boards also organize their digital governance activities with a technology and/or cybersecurity committee, and they make comprehensive disclosures on digital and cybersecurity risk. Grades are determined by applying the DiRECTOR framework in Appendix Exhibit 2 using qualitative data analysis techniques to assess relevant publicly available information (Zukis, 2021b). These self-regulated U.S. reforms mirror some of the leading practices identified in national codes and applied by companies in Malaysia and Nigeria.

The SEC is also ramping up its focus on accountability and has issued several enforcement actions related to cyber incident disclosure (Ferrillo *et al.*, 2021). Relying upon regulators and courts to establish standards after the fact is costly and inefficient. Many of the remediations that they force companies to enact in addition to fines and penalties mandate improvements in corporate governance over these issues and include reforms in director skills, boardroom structure and heightened accountability from the board and management on digital and cyber risk.

In 2022, the SEC has released proposed rules in cyber security that could significantly advance corporate governance and management practices for U.S. listed companies that builds upon their prior guidance in 2011 and 2018 (U.S. Securities and Exchange Commission, 2022). See Section 3.1 for a discussion of these proposed reforms.

The U.S. Congress has also proposed legal reforms on cyber expertise in the boardroom. Proposed federal Bill *S. 808 Cybersecurity Disclosure Act of 2021* would amend The Securities and Exchange Act of 1934 to require disclosing whether any governing body member has experience or expertise in cybersecurity (117th Congress, 2021). This proposed Bill has been reintroduced into the fourth straight U.S. Congress, demonstrating U.S. regulator's persistent efforts on mandating some basic corporate governance reform on these issues. This simple disclosure Bill would likely drive significant board reform. *S. 808* is similar to the reforms imposed with the Sarbanes-Oxley Act of 2002 when that

4.6. The United States

regulation mandated independent financial experts on public company audit committees.

The *National Institute of Standards and Technology* (NIST), a non-regulatory agency in the U.S. Department of Commerce, is America's leading standards body. NIST has been a thought leader in creating new principles and concepts related to systems security engineering and their application to complex digital systems. With *NIST SP 800-160 Vol 1 & Vol 2*, NIST is advancing a structured approach to systems thinking, design, and engineering to make complex systems more defensible and their risks survivable. First published in 2016, these comprehensive guidelines and tools build upon ISO/IEC 15288. In describing the need for a much more effective approach to these issues, they say (Ross et al., 2016):

> The need for trustworthy secure systems stems from a wide variety of *stakeholder* needs that are driven by mission, business, and a spectrum of other objectives and concerns. The characteristics of these systems include an ever-evolving growth in the geographic size, number, and types of *components* and technologies that compose the systems; the complexity and dynamicity in the interactions, behavior, and outcomes of systems and their system elements; and the increased dependence that results in *consequences* of major inconvenience to catastrophic loss due to disruptions, hazards, and threats within the global operating *environment*. The basic problem can be simply stated—today's systems have dimensions and an inherent complexity that require a disciplined and structured engineering approach to achieve any expectation that the inherent complexity can be effectively managed within the practical and feasible limits of human capability and certainty.

After the fact, well-known cyber-attacks such as Equifax and SolarWinds have also driven significant digital and cybersecurity governance reforms into these companies' boardrooms. However, proactive self-regulating digital governance reform is not happening at the pace it needs to be given the United States attractiveness as a digital target. Systemic risks in American businesses will also continue to increase and create large-scale economic, business, and social risks. While U.S. regulators are legislating more corporate accountability in data privacy and cybersecurity, they have not yet legislated more boardroom and director accountability. The SEC looks set to leapfrog existing approaches to cyber governance with their proposed rules.

4.7 International Organization for Standardization (ISO)

ISO is an independent, non-governmental federation of national standards bodies which shares knowledge and develops market-based and voluntary standards to solve global problems. They have a membership base comprised of 165 national standards bodies. ISO/IEC has two related standards that address digital and cybersecurity governance. Their information security-focused standard also addresses several critical issues related to systemic risk within the digital business system.

The current *ISO/IEC 38500* standard on information and communication governance is identical to the Australian standard. Initially, it was based upon the Australian *AS8015 Corporate Governance of Information and Communication Technology* standard created in 2005. The current second edition of ISO 38500 has a stated objective "... to provide principles, definitions, and a model for governing bodies to use when evaluating, directing, and monitoring the use of information technology (IT) in their organizations" (ISO/IEC, 2015, p. 5).

ISO/IEC 38500 is generally viewed as the leading international standard for digital governance. It is focused on opportunity risk, or the digital upside of how corporate governance over the application of information technology creates business value. In justifying the need for this governance standard, ISO/IEC explicitly acknowledges the poor return on investment that many companies experience with their substantial spending on IT as the reason why the standard is needed. They also address the most common source of these poor returns, "The main reasons for these negative outcomes are the emphasis on the technical, financial, and scheduling aspects of IT activities rather than emphasis on the whole business context of use of IT" (p. 5).

4.7. International Organization for Standardization (ISO)

This particular insight remains a common problem in governing information technology. The lack of leadership recognition that economies and businesses are already heavily dependent upon digital systems for much, if not most of the value that their economies and companies are creating remains a barrier to boardroom reform.

ISO/IEC 38500 lists a range of foundational benefits that develop from the effective corporate governance of IT:

- innovation in services, markets, and business;
- alignment of IT with business needs;
- appropriate implementation and operation of IT assets;
- clarity of responsibility and accountability for both the supply of and demand for IT in achieving the goals of the organization;
- business continuity and sustainability;
- efficient allocation of resources;
- good practice in relationships with stakeholders;
- actual realisation of the expected benefits from each IT investment; and
- assuring conformance with obligations (regulatory, legislation, contractual) concerning the acceptable use of IT (pp. 4–5)

The standard also integrates six-core behavioral principles intended to guide decision-making with a model focused on three main corporate governance tasks for directors to evaluate, direct and monitor the current and future use of IT. The standard is not intended to prescribe how IT governance should be applied but instead focuses on what should happen. The six principles address the need for corporate boards to ensure that the following objectives are being met:

> Responsibility: Ensure that IT accountabilities within the organization at the group and individual levels are understood, accepted, and executable.

Strategy: Make sure that the current and future IT capabilities are aligned to the changing strategic needs of the organization.

Acquisition: Have confidence that IT investments are supported by a balanced business case that addresses benefits, opportunities, costs, and risks over the short and long term that is monitored.

Performance: Ensures that IT performs at the service levels needed to meet current and future business requirements.

Conformance: Has confidence that IT complies with all legislation, regulations, and rules, and IT policies and practices are also defined, implemented, and enforced.

Human Behaviour: Understand and ensure that IT policies, practices, and decisions respect all human stakeholders' current and evolving needs.

The ISO standard is a simple and overarching framework that articulates the basic governance requirements for any governing body over IT. Focused mainly on digital risk and how the business strategically leverages and operationalizes information technologies, it does not encompass cybersecurity or systemic risks within modern IT systems. It is currently undergoing a scheduled five-year review.

A related ISO/IEC standard addresses the governance of information security risks. *ISO/IEC 27014:2020 Information security, cybersecurity and privacy protection — Governance of information security* offer boardrooms guidance for governing the digital downside. ISO/IEC 27014:2020 expects the board to take responsibility for the organization's effective information security management system.

Reflecting the same director tasks of evaluating, directing, and monitoring, the standard introduces the importance of communications in IT security governance by acknowledging the importance of cyber risk disclosure to interested parties such as shareholders. Emphasis is also included on the importance of the board receiving reliable and relevant reporting about information security activities. The timely and accurate disclosure of cyber risks and incidents is essential in protecting investor interests and is becoming a focus and enforcement cudgel for regulators in the United States.

ISO/IEC 27014:2020 also addresses several issues related to the board's governance of systemic risk. Explicitly stated is a systemic risk-based information security governance objective focused on "preventing the organization's information technology from being used to harm other organizations" (ISO/IEC 27014 2nd edition 2020–12, 2020, p. 4). Other tasks placed squarely on the governance function by the standard include defining risk appetite, approving information security strategy, and promoting a positive information security culture.

The standard also explicitly addresses the need to govern situations where a third party could manage the information security function. This systemic risk issue can relate to situations where a managed service provider is outsourcing a security function, or a third-party provides a service such as cloud computing capability, e.g., Amazon Web Services. Notably, the standard also emphasizes the need to understand the scope of information security related to systemically essential issues such as external requirements, interfaces, and other dependencies. Adopting a risk-based approach to information security is also a focal point of the standard whereas a technical approach is still commonly applied and is the focus of many boardroom communications from IT management teams.

The ISO/IEC standards are comprehensive and leading global frameworks that can be readily adopted by any corporate boardroom or governing body to guide their approach to digital and cybersecurity governance.

4.8 The DiRECTOR Framework for Systemic Risk Governance

The DiRECTOR framework is a qualitative systemic risk assessment framework designed for corporate boards to help them understand and govern systemic risk in complex digital business systems, see Exhibit 2 (Zukis, 2019). Developed by the author, DiRECTOR complements the ISO standards by providing structure and a qualitative framework to analyze systemic issues that drive digital value creation and protection.

A stakeholder value-aligned framework, DiRECTOR identifies the eight-core domains inherent within every digital business system that need to work together for the system to fulfill the purposes for which it was designed and built. DiRECTOR aims to improve the understanding and recognition of systemic risk and how the parts of a digital business system work together to create and protect value for all stakeholders.

The framework also incorporates the five core elements that contribute to systemic risk levels within complex digital business systems. The framework was developed based upon research into the evolution of the international regulatory accord named Basel III that started in 2009 after the 2008 financial markets driven recession. The five essential elements that drive systemic risk into complex digital business systems are replaceability, inter-connectedness, size, complexity, and the x-jurisdictional requirements upon and between the parts of any complex systems (Zukis *et al.*, 2022). By identifying and assessing these issues across each of the eight DiRECTOR domains through the lens of these five forces of systemic risk, corporate leaders are gaining a better understanding of systemic risks inherent within digital business systems.

Corporate directors and technology executives are applying DiRECTOR to create a common language around systemic risk related to the digital business system and to introduce a structured approach to understanding, identifying, governing and managing systemic risk. DiRECTOR and its eight domains also provide a useful model for assessing digitally savvy director competencies, the alignment of boardroom structure and responsibility within committee charters on digital and cybersecurity governance, and the scope of digital and cybersecurity risk disclosures.

5

Recommended Digital and Cybersecurity Governance Reforms

At present, developments in national codes and leading practices are relying upon self-regulatory initiative to shape existing boardroom practices in digital and cybersecurity oversight. The leading practices that are emerging are focused on director skills, board structure, and the scope of risk oversight with particular acknowledgement of and emphasis on systemic cyber risk. These comprehensive, albeit voluntary, global digital governance frameworks have existed for over a decade and are helpful starting points for any boardroom wanting to initiate a more effective corporate governance approach to these issues.

However, digital risks continue to grow at a rate far exceeding the pace of self-regulatory boardroom reform in cybersecurity. While legal and regulatory mandates in corporate governance are on the horizon, boardroom reform in digital and cyber risk oversight needs to be accelerated to drive faster corporate governance transformation. Suggested legal reforms for regulators and leading practice improvements are recommended below in three principal areas: director skills, boardroom structure, and risk disclosure.

5.1 Digital Diversity Quotas and Digital Skills Disclosure

Legal reforms are needed in boardroom cyber expertise. Boardroom gender diversity quotas have shown that legislative action can drive a faster rate of boardroom reform in director composition (National Women's Council, 2021). Digital and cybersecurity governance effectiveness starts with digitally savvy corporate directors. The critical mass correlation identified by MIT between business results and the presence of three digitally savvy directors on a board supports the need for much more digital diversity in the corporate boardroom than exists at present.

Legal reform is needed to drive digital and cyber director capabilities onto corporate boards more quickly and broadly. Legal reform to corporate governance related laws should initially address the urgent need to have cybersecurity expertise and experience on corporate boards. Current proposed SEC rules and the Bill being proposed in the United States Senate to require disclosure of boardroom cyber expertise is the blueprint for this legal reform. Either of these legal reforms will amend The Securities and Exchange Act of 1934 if passed into law and require covered companies to disclose whether any member of the board has cybersecurity experience or expertise. Effective digital and cybersecurity governance is not possible without the boardroom skills to understand these issues. Protecting the enormous amount of economic and business value already being enabled by complex digital business systems is the starting point for foundational digital and cybersecurity governance reform and requires the certainty and urgency created by legal mandate. Listing standards worldwide, or other related corporate laws should reflect this foundational need for both public and private companies.

Additional "soft" self-regulatory reforms should focus on updates to national corporate governance codes that drive digital diversity breadth into the boardroom to reflect the comprehensive capabilities needed to govern the totality of the digital business system. Recommendations should be added to national codes for detailed disclosure of director digital expertise. Some leading digital governance practices in the U.S. already identify director competencies in data, information architecture, risk communications, emerging technology, cybersecurity, IT operations, and regulatory experience.

Following the lead of Malaysia firm Maybank, we believe national codes should also recommend the disclosure of director training received during the year and the nature of director education programs in these areas. Identifying expertise and digital and cyber literacy of corporate directors is a key step in advancing director professionalism and performance on these issues.

5.2 Board Structure and a Technology and Cybersecurity Committee

"Soft" reforms should be made in how corporate boards organize their activities and responsibilities in governing digital and cyber risk. Committee structures drive a focused approach to the issues being governed, bring more accountability, and send a strong internal and external signal. The frequent approach of conducting cybersecurity risk oversight through an audit committee introduces a range of problems ranging from the likely misalignment of director skills to the marginalization of the cybersecurity risk oversight agenda.

A "soft" reform approach to committee structure is recommended with an update to national corporate governance codes in countries around the world and through regulatory guidance and leading practice identification. With "comply and explain" or more explanatory principles in place within many national codes, a self-regulated reform will enable corporate boards some flexibility in committee design. However, this will nonetheless hold corporate boards to the higher standard by requiring an explanation of how the board has made the decisions it has made to organize corporate governance activities to effectively govern the full digital and cybersecurity governance agenda.

Updated national codes should recommend the leading practice of a technology and cybersecurity committee. This would place a fourth committee alongside the common requirement or practice of a standing audit committee, nominating committee, and remuneration committee. Governing the digital upside alongside its downside in a technology and cybersecurity committee is already a leading practice that adds efficiencies and effectiveness to the oversight of these issues.

This is recommended as a "soft" reform even though it is a leading practice because other committees such as a risk management committee can incorporate these responsibilities through their charter. This reform allows boards to be transparent and thoughtful with their organizational approach by explaining how the same scope of oversight is achieved with a different committee design. Ensuring active governance of the comprehensive digital and cybersecurity agenda is the primary goal, and committee design is secondary.

5.3 Cyber and Systemic Risk Disclosure

Legal reform is needed in cyber and systemic risk disclosure, not self-regulatory guidance. Cyber-attack strategies and tactics evolve and emerge quickly, faster than the ability of defenders to launch protective countermeasures. Attackers have shifted their strategy from monetizing the data they exfiltrate on secondary markets to now holding companies, critical processes, and the public interest hostage. The "crown jewel" for every company and organization is its ability to function, i.e., to transact; to move fuel through a pipeline; to keep the lights on. Attackers are now attacking the ability of digital economies and general economies to function.

Systemic risk is the risk that exists between the parts of a complex connected system and is a new challenge in enterprise risk management. The growing complexity and inter-connectedness of digital economies creates new risks. With the growing complexity of digital systems, attackers have figured out that the system itself is the weak point. Attackers are now exploiting these complex systems with attacks targeted at their systemic weak points, such as the SolarWinds attack.

Incident and risk disclosure reforms are needed in cybersecurity and systemic risk disclosure to ensure that investors have a useful explanation of the systemic risk environment inherent with the company and throughout the ecosystem the company functions within. Management teams need to do much more work in understanding systemic risk and boardroom accountability on this issue will drive immediate progress.

"Soft" expectations in the United States from the SEC already address cyber risk disclosure, but experience has shown this suggested

5.3. Cyber and Systemic Risk Disclosure

guidance to be ineffective. India has recently introduced mandated reforms in place for incident disclosure in its ICT industry to reduce the spread of systemic risks. Suggestive guidance does not go far enough and has not resulted in the quality of disclosure required to inform investors effectively. Moreover, systemic risk disclosure related to the digital business system is virtually non-existent in the United States. These indications suggest that these risks are not yet well understood by boards and management teams.

Understanding cyber risk materiality requires an understanding of the financial impacts of cyber risk. While disclosure of the financial amount of expected cyber losses is too prescriptive, which could be helpful information for attackers, disclosure of a company's assessment and monitoring program overseeing projected cyber economic losses is relevant information for investors. These disclosures would provide investors with helpful information that allows them to understand the maturity of the practices and policies being deployed to govern and manage the organization's self-insured cyber risk levels.

Legal reform in systemic risk disclosure should focus on the organization's specific systemic risk environment and how management is monitoring and mitigating systemic risk. A minimum disclosure should qualitatively address non-generic issues in the digital business system and the organization's systemic risk environment, including the approach and methodology used to assess and monitor systemic risks.

Explicit legal reforms should also require that boards receive an independent third-party assessment of cybersecurity programs and of the organization's systemic risk levels. Accounting rules should also be updated to address the need to account for projected cyber losses that are probable and can be estimated. Disclosure reforms are vital to investors, and also offer a useful defense for companies to the growing amount of litigation risk in these areas. Ultimately however, understanding these risks leads to a more effective approach in managing them and reducing them and that is the goal.

6

Conclusions

Corporate boards and directors worldwide have a duty and responsibility to govern and understand digital and cybersecurity risks. Investors, customers, and other stakeholders are paying the price for the slow adoption of digital and cybersecurity risk oversight policies and practices.

The need for corporate governance reform in digital and cybersecurity risk oversight is worldwide. New cyber risks and systemic threats are introducing new dangers to economies and businesses alike. The companies that have shown digital boardroom leadership have demonstrated positive differentiated business results in revenue growth, profitability, return on assets, and market capitalization. Boardroom leadership and effective digital and cyber governance on these issues has a material business and economic impact.

Well-developed and applied leading practices and standards are currently available to voluntary enable digital and cybersecurity board reform. While this type of self-regulated digital boardroom reform is occurring, it is the exception, not the rule. Legislative reform is urgently needed to advance corporate governance practices and policies worldwide in response to this significant and evolving risk.

Legislative reform that requires competent directors capable to govern these issues with digital director quotas will support national digital mandates, investor and public interests, and national security interests. Legislative quotas for digitally savvy directors must first address the acute need for cybersecurity expertise in the boardroom. Legal reform is also needed to mandate this core boardroom competency to drive much faster board transformation.

"Soft" reforms in self-regulatory codes and practices are suggested in boardroom organizing principles around digital and cybersecurity risk. But legal reforms are needed in cyber and systemic risk disclosure to better inform investors, and ultimately drive more effective systemic risk reduction practices.

Boardrooms and their corporate directors are critical parts of the complex system that powers every company's digital future and every country's digital destiny. Digital economies need high-performing digital businesses and digitally effective boardrooms. Boards and policymakers need to drive faster corporate governance reform on these issues to protect stakeholder, investor, and national interests.

The development of digital and cyber governance policies and practices is long overdue. This monograph documents and illustrates the state of these issues where practices and policies are emerging to assemble a body of representative and actionable guidelines and tactics. Any corporate board around the world currently has the ability to self-regulate their way to an effective approach in governing digital and cyber risk. Corporate governance reform will reduce real levels of business risk while also driving digital transformation and its many benefits.

Appendix

Exhibit 1

Job Summary:

The Chief Information Officer will develop, plan, and implement an information technology (IT) strategy that meets the company's business needs, delivers optimal return on investment, and maintains utmost security.

Supervisory Responsibilities:

- Oversees projects and assignments within the Information Systems (IS) department.

- Leads efficient operation of the team so that prompt modernization and upgrades of IS are performed as needed.

- Conducts performance evaluations that are timely and constructive.

Duties/Responsibilities:

- Collaborates with members of the executive team to identify ways IT can assist the company in achieving business and financial goals.

- Identifies new IS developments and technologies; anticipates resulting organizational modifications.

- Ensures that IT and network infrastructure adequately support the company's computing, data processing, and communications needs.

- Develops and implements the IT budget.

- Communicates goals, projects, and timelines of the company to the department; plans ways to execute those goals within the department.

- Establishes long-term IS needs and plans and develops strategies for developing systems and acquiring software and hardware necessary to meet those needs.

- Assists as top-level contact for end users in determining IS requirements and/or solutions.

- Ensures compliance with government regulations that apply to systems operations.

- Performs other related duties as assigned.

Required Skills/Abilities:

- Excellent verbal and written communication skills.

- Proficient in Microsoft Office Suite or related software.

- Excellent ability to conceptualize long-term business goals and develop orderly processes to accomplish those goals.

- Excellent managerial skills (SHRM, 2021).

Exhibit 2

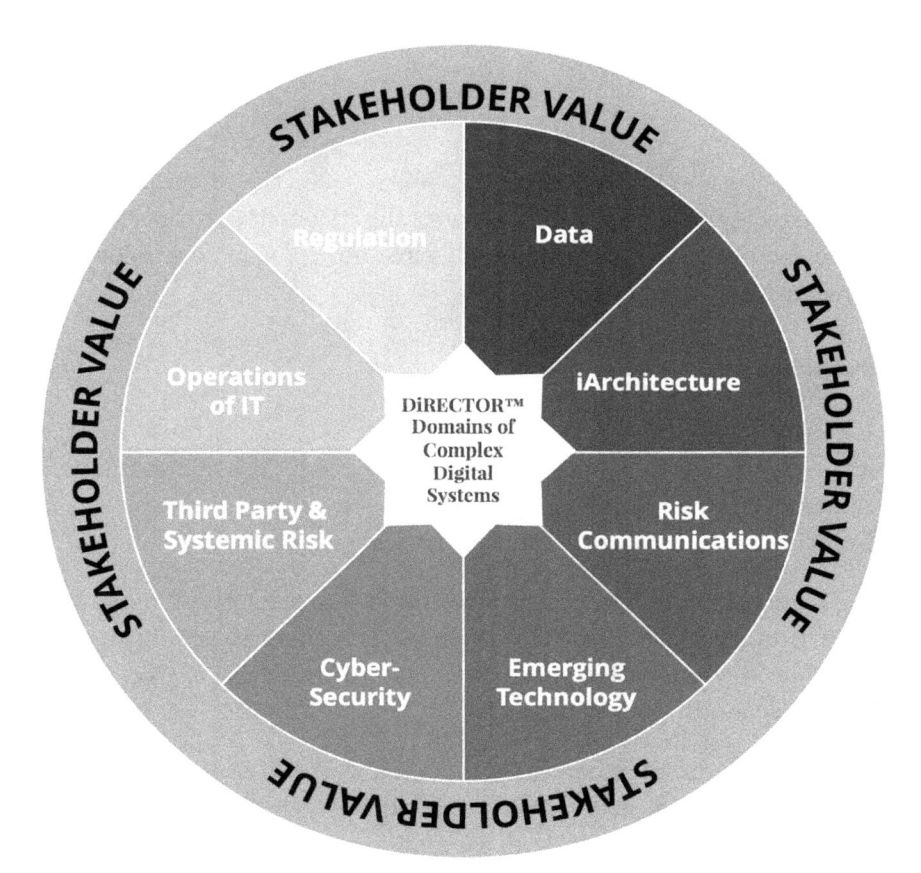

Figure A.1: The DiRECTOR framework for qualitatively assessing systemic risk in complex digital business systems.

Source: Digital Directors Network (2019).

Exhibit 3

Leading Practices Boardroom Technology and Cybersecurity Committee Charter

Purpose

The Technology and Cybersecurity Committee (the "Committee") is appointed by the Board of Directors (the "Board") to provide oversight and counsel on matters relating to information technology and cybersecurity risk oversight.

Responsibilities

The basic responsibility of the members of the Committee is to act in what they reasonably believe to be in the best interests of the Company, its shareholders, and stakeholders. In discharging that obligation, the Committee has the following authority and responsibilities:

(1) To review and discuss the overall strategy of the Company as it pertains to digital and cybersecurity governance, in order to make recommendations to the Board on strategies, operations and related issues regarding:

 (i) Trends in information technology that could significantly affect the competitive position of the Company and the industries in which it operates and the creation of digital and business value.

 (ii) Emerging technologies, device management, and investment in information technology hardware and software lifecycle management.

 (iii) The architecture of the digital business system and related risks and opportunities.

 (iv) Monitoring cyber threat intelligence and cyber threat risk mitigation and ensuring business continuity and recovery in the event of a cyber breach.

(v) The projected economic impacts of cyber risk including the Company's self-insured exposure and the strategies and tactics to transfer this risk, mitigate it or accept it.

(vi) Systemic risk within the digital business system and issues related to inbound and outbound systemic risks that could impact the company or others, including third-party IT risk management

(vii) Data and information lifecycle management, including data privacy issues.

(viii) IT portfolio project management and IT services delivery.

(ix) Social media monitoring and risk management.

(x) Digital and cybersecurity regulatory issues, requirements, and potential fines.

(xi) Operations of IT including staffing, retention, performance, and development, including enterprise-wide awareness, preparedness programs, internal and third-party risk communications, and incident response.

(2) To track and measure the relationship between the Company's digital and cybersecurity governance mechanisms and its performance, competitive position, prospects for growth, overall digital risk profile, and business value at stake.

(3) To set risk tolerances and assess and monitor risk appetite for digital investments and strategies that drive and support business value.

(4) To carry out other activities consistent with this Charter, the Bylaws, and applicable laws that the Committee or the Board may deem necessary or appropriate.

Committee Members

The Committee will consist of at least three Board members, as appointed annually by the Board on the recommendation of the Nominating and Governance Committee. Each member of the Committee will serve a one-year term or until his or her earlier resignation, removal, or death. At least two Committee members will be independent Qualified Technology Experts (QTE) who have significant familiarity and experience with information technology or technology transformation and cybersecurity matters, as shown to the Board by way of educational background and demonstrated relevancy of skills and competencies including relevant field experience. At least one Committee member will be a cybersecurity expert with the requisite cybersecurity field expertise needed by the Company to oversee the protection of business value.

Chairperson

The Chairperson of the Committee will be a Qualified Technology Expert (QTE) or cybersecurity expert. The Chairperson will be an Independent Director appointed by the Nominating and Governance Committee of the Board and may be removed by the Board at any time, with or without cause. If the Chairperson is not available to perform his/her responsibilities or attend a Committee meeting, the Chairperson will temporarily delegate his/her responsibilities to an acting chair.

Meetings

The Committee will meet as often as it determines appropriate or necessary, at a minimum of four times per year. The Chairperson of the Committee will preside at each meeting and may direct appropriate management and staff members to prepare draft agendas and background information for each meeting. The Chairperson will review and approve any draft agenda and distribute it to the Committee at least one day before the meeting. All meetings of the Committee will be held per the Bylaws of the Company, and written minutes of each meeting, in the form approved by the Committee, will be filed in the Company records. In the absence of the Chairperson of the Committee, an acting chair will review and distribute the agenda and any background materials to members at least one day in advance of the meeting. The Chairperson of the Committee (or acting chair) will report to the Board on matters addressed at the Committee meeting at its subsequent meeting, including quarterly reports on economic exposures of cyber risk and the Company's cybersecurity risk profile. The Committee may include members of the Company's management, other members of the Board, or third parties in its meetings.

Oversight

The Committee may delegate authority to subcommittees consisting of one or more Committee members when appropriate. The Committee has the power to retain outside experts or advisors to carry out its responsibilities. It has the sole authority to approve the fees and retention terms of any such individuals at the Company's expense. The Committee will evaluate the fulfillment of its responsibilities, review its charter, and recommend any proposed changes to the Nominating and Governance Committee and the Board for review and approval annually (Digital Directors Network, 2021b).

References

117th Congress (2021). *S. 808 Cybersecurity Disclosure Act of 2021*. URL: https://www.congress.gov/bill/117th-congress/senate-bill/808/text.

Accenture (2022). *Global Incident Report: Russia-Ukraine Crisis | April 21*. Accenture.

Ang, C. (2021). *The Most Significant Cyber Attacks from 2006–2020, by Country*. URL: https://www.visualcapitalist.com/cyber-attacks-worldwide-2006-2020/.

Bayarma, A., C. Hubers, T. Schwanen, and D. E. Martin Dijst (2011). "Anything, anywhere, anytime? Developing indicators to assess the spatial and temporal fragmentation of activities (Alexander Anything Spatial and Temporal Relevance, P. 1: 1250)". *Environment and Planning*: 678–705.

BNP Media (2020). *Security*. (B. Media, Producer) Security: URL: https://www.securitymagazine.com/articles/93062-ransomware-victim-travelex-forced-into-bankruptcy.

Bordoff, J. (2021). *Foreign Policy Voice*. URL: https://foreignpolicy.com/2021/05/17/colonial-pipeline-crisis-cyberattack-ransomware-cybersecurity-energy-electicity-power-grid-russia-hackers/.

Braue, D. (2021). *ACS Information Age*. ACS Information Age: URL: https://ia.acs.org.au/article/2021/hold-company-directors-liable-for-cyber-attacks.html.

Brynjolfsson, E. and A. McAfee (2011). *Race Against the Matchine: How the Digital Revolution is Accelerating Innovation, Driving Productivity, and Irreversibly Transforming Emplyoment and the Economy.* Lexington, Massachusetts, USA: Digital Frontier Press.

Chakravorti, B., R. Shankar Chaturvedi, C. Filipovic, and G. Brewer (2020). *Digital in the Time of Covid: Trust in the Digital Economy and Its Evolution Across 90 Economies As the Planet Paused for a Pandemic.* Medford, MA: The Fletcher School at Tufts Unviersity.

Chen, K. D. and A. Wu (2016). *The Structure of Board Committees.* Boston: Harvard Business School.

CMS Law (2022). *Enforcement Tracker.* GDPR Enforcement Tracker: URL: https://www.enforcementtracker.com/?insights.

CNA Financial Corporation (2021). "Form 10-Q". In: *Quarterly Report Pursuant to Section 13 or 15(d) of the Securities Exchange Act of 1934.* Chicago, IL, USA.

Commonwealth of Australia (2021). *Strengthening Australia's Cyber Security Regulations and Incentives—A Call for Views.* Commonwealth of Australia.

Cyentia Institute LLC (2020). *IRIS 20/20 Extreme: Analyzing the 100 Largest Cyber Loss Events of the Last Five Years.* Cyentia Institute LLC.

Dezan Shira & Associates (2021). *The PRC Personal Information Protection Law (Final): A Full Translation.* URL: https://www.china-briefing.com/news/the-prc-personal-information-protection-law-final-a-full-translation/.

Digital Directors Network (2019). Systemic Digital Risk: Understanding and Overseeing Complex Digital Environments with the DiRECTOR™ and RISCX™ Frameworks.

Digital Directors Network (2021a). Boardroom Solutions: URL: https://www.digitaldirectors.network/cpages/briefings.

Digital Directors Network (2021b). *Digital Governance Maturity Model.* Los Angeles: DDN LLC.

Dittmar, J. (2011). *Information technology and economic change: The impact of the printing press.* voxeu.org: URL: https://voxeu.org/article/information-technology-and-economic-change-impact-printing-press.

Eaton, C. and D. Volz (2021). *Colonial Pipeline CEO Tells Why He Paid Hackers a $4.4 Million Ransom.* URL: https://www.wsj.com/articles/colonial-pipeline-ceo-tells-why-he-paid-hackers-a-4-4-million-ransom-11621435636.

Eddy, M. and N. Perlroth (2020). *Cyber Attack Suspected in German Woman's Death.* The New York Times: URL: https://www.nytimes.com/2020/09/18/world/europe/cyber-attack-germany-ransomware-death.html.

European Commission (2020). *Joint Communication to the European Parliament and the Council: The EU's Cybersecurity Strategy for the Digital Decade.* Brussels: European Commission.

FASB of the Financial Accounting Foundation (2010). *FASB Exposure Draft Proposed Accounting Standards Update Contingencies (Topic 450).* FASB.

Federal Trade Commission (2019). *FTC Imposes $5 Billion Penalty and Sweeping New Privacy Restrictions on Facebook.* URL: https://www.ftc.gov/news-events/press-releases/2019/07/ftc-imposes-5-billion-penalty-sweeping-new-privacy-restrictions.

FedEx Corporation (2022). *FORM–10K.* Memphis: FedEx Corporation.

Ferrillo, P., B. Zukis, and C. Veltsos (2021). *The SEC's Clear Reminder About the Need for Quality Cybersecurity Disclosures.* URL: https://corpgov.law.harvard.edu/contributor/bob-zukis/.

Financial Reporting Council of Nigeria (2018). *Nigerian Code of Corporate Governance 2018.* Financial Reporting Council of Nigeria Act.

Financial Stability Board (2020). *2020 list of global systemically important banks.* URL: https://www.fsb.org/2020/11/2020-list-of-global-systemically-important-banks-g-sibs/.

Galloway, A. (2021). *'Real and Present Danger:' Government considers making company directors personally liable for cyber attacks.* The Sydney Morning Herald: URL: https://www.smh.com.au/politics/federal/real-and-present-danger-government-considers-making-company-directors-personally-liable-for-cyber-attacks-20210712-p588vz.html.

Gomez, B. (2021). Vice President, Equilar. (B. Zukis, Interviewer).

Greig, J. (2022). *Bridgestone still struggling with plant closures across North America after cyberattack.* ZD Net: URL: https://www.zdnet.com/article/bridgestone-still-struggling-with-plant-closures-after-cyberattack/.

Guaranty Trust Bank plc. (2021). *2020 Annual Report.* Lagos: Guaranty Trust Bank plc.

Hasbro, Inc. (2020). *Form 10-K.* Rhode Island: Hasbro, Inc.

Haverstock, E. (2021). *Inside The Global 2000: The Value of the World's Largest Public Companies Soars, As Sales And Profits Falter.* Forbes.Com: URL: https://www.forbes.com/sites/elizahaverstock/2021/05/13/inside-the-global-2000-the-value-of-the-worlds-largest-public-companies-soar-as-sales-and-profits-falter/?sh=1d8369aa26d4.

Hawkins, A. J. (2022). *Toyota shuts down its Japanese factories after reported cyberattack.* URL: https://www.theverge.com/2022/2/28/22954688/toyota-cyberattack-factory-shut-down-cars-output.

Ho, J. (2021). *Corporate boards: Don't underestimate your role in data security oversight.* Contrary to popular belief, data security begins with the Board of Directors, not the IT Department.

Hope, A. (2021). *Cyber Insurance Firm Suffers Sophisticated Ransomware Cyber Attack; Data Obtained May Help Hackers Better Target Firm's Customers.* URL: https://www.cpomagazine.com/cyber-security/cyber-insurance-firm-suffers-sophisticated-ransomware-cyber-attack-data-obtained-may-help-hackers-better-target-firms-customers/.

Huang, K., R. Ye, and S. Madnick (2019). *Both Sides of the Coin: The Impact of Cyber Attacks on Business Value.* Cambridge: MIT Sloan School of Management.

Huawei and Oxford Economics (2017). *Digital Spillover—Measuring the True Impact of the Digital Economy.* Shenzen: Huawei Technologies Co., Ltd.

IBM Security (2021). *Cost of a Data Breach Report 2021.* IBM.

IDC (2020). *IDC FutureScape: Worldwide Digital Transformation Predictions 2021.* Framingham: IDC.

Insitute of Directors Southern Africa KING IV (2016). *Draft King IV Report—Responses to the summarised public comments 2016.* Insitute of Directors Southern Africa.

Institute of Directors In Southern Africa NPC (2016). *KING IV Report On Corporate Governanace For Southern Africa.* Johannesburg: Institute of Directors In Southern Africa NPC.

Institutional Investor (2021). *Japan's Corporate Governance Code Revised in Anticipation of "Prime Market" Segment Coming to TSE.* URL: https://www.institutionalinvestor.com/article/b1spy621t219 ny/Japan-s-Corporate-Governance-Code-Revised-in-Anticipation -of-Prime-Market-Segment-Coming-to-TSE.

International Monetary Fund (2018). *Measuring The Digital Economy.* Washington, D.C.: International Monetary Fund.

International Organization Of Securities Commissions (2021). *Environmental, Social and Governance (ESG) Ratings and Data Products Providers.* Madrid: International Organization Of Securities Commissions.

International Telecommunication Union (2018). *Assessing the Economic Impact of Artificial Intelligence.* Geneva: International Telecommunication Union.

ISO/IEC (2015). *Internation Standard ISO/IEC 38500 2nd edition Information technology-Governance of IT for the organization.* Geneva: ICO/IEC.

ISO/IEC 27014 2nd edition 2020–12 (2020). *Information security, cybersecurity and privacy protection — Governance of information security (ISO_IEC_27014_2020(en). P. 1:0).* Geneva: ISO/IEC.

ISO/IEC/IEEE 15288 (2015). *Systems and software engineering—System life cycle processes.* First edn. Geneva and New York: ISO/IEC/IEEE.

ISS (2021). *Governance QualityScore.* URL: https://www.issgovernance.com/esg/ratings/governance-qualityscore/.

Jones Day (2021). *China Finalizes Data Security Law to Strengthen Regulation on Data Protection.* URL: https://www.jdsupra.com/legalnews/china-finalizes-data-security-law-to-4249871/.

Lee, C. (2021). *Vietnam digital economy expected to contribute 20 percent of GDP by 2025*. URL: https://vietnamtimes.org.vn/vietnam-digital-economy-expected-to-contribute-20-percent-of-gdp-by-2025-21229.html.

Lewis, M. J. (2020). "Independent Directors Mitigate Legal Risk". *Private Company Director*: 56.

Malayan Banking Berhad (2020). *Corporate Governance Report*. Kuala Lumpur: Malayan Banking Berhad.

Marsh & McLennan Companies Ltd. Inc. and Global Network of Director Institutes (2021). *Global Network of Directors Institutes 2020–2021 Survey Report*. Marsh & McLennan Companies Ltd, Inc. | Global Network of Director Institutes.

Mehrotra, K. and W. Turton (2021). *CNA Paid $40 Million in Ransom After March Cyber Attack*. URL: https://www.insurancejournal.com/news/national/2021/05/21/615373.htm.

Morgan, S. (2020). *Cybercrime Magazine*. Cybercrime Magazine: URL: https://cybersecurityventures.com/hackerpocalypse-cybercrime-report-2016/.

Munter, P. (2021). *Statement on OCA's Continued Focus on High Quality Financial Reporting in a Complex Environment*. URL: https://www.sec.gov/news/statement/munter-oca-2021-12-06.

MyLogIQ (2021). *S&P 500 and R3000 Technology and Cybersecurity Oversight*. San Juan: MyLogIQ.

National Center for Incident Readiness and Strategy for Cybersecurity (2021). *Outline of Japan's Next Cybersecurity Strategy*. NISC: URL: https://www.nisc.go.jp/eng/.

National Women's Council (2021). *Increasing Gender Balance on Boards: The case for Legislative Gender Quotas in Ireland*. Dublin: National Women's Council.

Neuberger, A. (2021). *White House*. White House: URL: https://www.whitehouse.gov/wp-content/uploads/2021/06/Memo-What-We-Urge-You-To-Do-To-Protect-Against-The-Threat-of-Ransomware.pdf.

New York State Department of Financial Services (2021). *Insurance Circular Letter No. 2*. URL: https://www.dfs.ny.gov/industry_guidance/circular_letters/cl2021_02.

References

OECD (2015). *G20/OECD Principles of Corporate Governance*. Paris: OECD Publishing.

Panettieri, J. (2021). *SolarWinds Orion Security Breach: Cyberattack Timeline and Hacking Incident Details*. URL: https://www.channele2e.com/technology/security/solarwinds-orion-breach-hacking-incident-timeline-and-updated-details/4/.

Patterson Balknap Webb and Tyler, LLP. (2021). *SEC Signals Renewed Interest in Cybersecurity Disclosure Enforcement*. URL: https://www.jdsupra.com/legalnews/sec-signals-renewed-interest-in-6695892/.

Perez, S. (2021). *Walmart to sell it's e-commerce technologies to other retailers*. TechCrunch.com: URL: https://techcrunch.com/2021/07/28/walmart-to-sell-its-e-commerce-technologies-to-other-retailers/.

Powell, J. (2021). 60 Minutes. URL: https://www.cbsnews.com/news/jerome-powell-full-2021-60-minutes-interview-transcript/ (S. Pelley, Interviewer).

Pritchard, S. (2022). *India to introduce six-hour data breach notification rule*. URL: https://portswigger.net/daily-swig/india-to-introduce-six-hour-data-breach-notification-rule.

Reuters (2021a). *Business: AIG is reducing cyber insurance limits as cost of coverage soars*. URL: https://www.reuters.com/business/aig-is-reducing-cyber-insurance-limits-cost-coverage-soars-2021-08-06/.

Reuters (2021b). *Revisions of Japan's Corporate Governance Code and Guidelines for Investor and Company Engagement*. Tokyo: The Council of Experts Concerning the Follow-up of Japan's Stewardship Code and Japan's Corporate Governance Code.

Ross, R., M. McEvilley, and J. Carrier Oren (2016). *Systems Security Engineering Considerations for a Multidisciplinary Approach in the Engineering of Trustworthy Secure Systems*. Gaithersburg: U.S. Department of Commerce/National Institute of Standards and Technology.

Securities Commission Malaysia (2021). *Malaysian Code on Corporate Governance (as at 28 April 2021)*. Kuala Lumpur: Securities Commission Malaysia.

Shoprite Holdings Ltd. (2020). *Application of the King IV Code Principles*. Johannesburg: Shoprite Holdings Ltd.

SHRM (2021). *Job Description Chief Information Officer*. URL: https://www.shrm.org/ResourcesAndTools/tools-and-samples/job-descriptions/Pages/Chief-Information-Officer.aspx.

SpencerStuart (2017). *Boardroom Best Practice: Lessons learned from board assessments across Europe*. SpencerStuart.

The Hindu (2021). *Government to unveil national cyber security strategy soon: National Cyber Security Coordinator*. URL: https://www.thehindu.com/business/government-to-unveil-national-cyber-security-strategy-soon-national-cyber-security-coordinator/article35119538.ece.

The White House (2022). *Office of the National Cyber Director*. The White House: URL: https://www.whitehouse.gov/oncd/.

Tricor Group and FT Board Director Programme (2021). *2021 Asia Pacific Board Director Barometer Report*. Hong Kong: Tricor Group.

Turton, W. and K. Mehrotra (2021). *Hackers Breached Colonial Pipeline Using Compromised Password*. URL: https://www.bloomberg.com/news/articles/2021-06-04/hackers-breached-colonial-pipeline-using-compromised-password.

UNCTAD (2019). *Digital Economy Report 2019 Value Creation And Capture: Implications For Developing Countries*. New York: United Nations.

U.S. Bureau of Economic Analysis (2021). *Updated Digital Economy Estimates*, U.S. Bureau of Economic Analysis. Washington, D.C.: U.S. Bureau of Economic Analysis (BEA).

U.S. Securities and Exchange Commission (2021). *Cybersecurity Risk Governance*. URL: https://www.reginfo.gov/public/do/eAgendaViewRule?pubId=202104&RIN=3235-AM89.

U.S. Securities and Exchange Commission (2022a). March 9. *SEC Proposes Rules on Cybersecurity Risk Management, Strategy, Governance, and Incident Disclosure by Public Companies*. URL: https://www.sec.gov/news/press-release/2022-39.

U.S. Securities and Exchange Commission (2022b). *Cybersecurity Risk Management, Strategy, Governance, and Incident Disclosure File No. S7-09-22*. Washingto, DC: Securities and Exchange Commission.

Walmart Inc. (2021). *Form 10-K*. Bentonville: Walmart Inc.

Weill, P., T. Apel, S. L. Woerner, and J. S. Banner (2019). *Assessing The Impact Of A Digitially Savvy Board On Company Performance*. Boston: MIT Management Sloan School Center For Information Systems Research (CISR).

World Economic Forum (2019). *Our Shared Digital Future Responsible Digital Transformation—Board Briefing*. Geneva: World Economic Forum.

Zukis, B. (2016). *Are Cyber Experts On Boards Inevitable?* URL: https://www.conference-board.org/blog/postdetail.cfm?post=5917.

Zukis, B. (2019). *DDN Releases DiRECTOR The Only Systemic Risk Framework Focused On Complex Digital Systems*. URL: https://www.digitaldirectors.network/blogs/ddn-releases-director-the-only-systemic-risk-framework-focused-on-complex-digital-systems.

Zukis, B. (2020). *Ransomware Has A New And Very Valuable Hostage In Sight*. URL: https://www.forbes.com/sites/bobzukis/2020/06/18/ransomware-has-a-new-and-very-valuable-hostage-in-sight/?sh=2f8ba91d170f.

Zukis, B. (2021a). *China, Fred Astaire And The Countries Dancing Towards The Digital Future*. URL: https://www.forbes.com/sites/bobzukis/2021/07/21/china-fred-astaire-and-the-countries-dancing-towards-the-digital-future/?sh=147ed10e6394.

Zukis, B. (2021b). "The Boardrooms Leading America's Digital Transformation". *NACD Directorship*: 24–30.

Zukis, B. (2022). *The SEC Is About To Force CISOs Into America's Boardrooms*. URL: https://www.forbes.com/sites/bobzukis/2022/04/18/the-sec-is-about-to-force-cisos-into-americas-boardrooms/?sh=7e7bf1ed68a9.

Zukis, B., P. Ferrillo, and C. Veltsos (2022). *The Great Reboot—Succeeding in a Complex Digital World Under Attack From Systemic Risk*. 2nd edn. Los Angeles: DDN Press.